Choosing HONOR

Choosing HONOR

An American Woman's Search for God, Family and Country in an Age of Corruption

Mary T. Ficalora

AVAIL PRESS

Choosing Honor
An American Woman's Search for God, Family and Country in an Age of Corruption

Thousand Oaks, CA
www.availpress.com

All rights reserved. No part of this book may be reproduced or transmitted in any form or by any means, electronic or mechanical, without written permission from the author.

Developmental Editor: Virginia Crane
Copy Editor: Melanie Rigney
Cover Design by George Foster
Interior Design by William Groetzinger

Copyright © 2008 by Mary T. Ficalora

ISBN 978-0-9799359-1-6
Library of Congress Control Number: 2008900065

Publishers Cataloging-in-Publication
(Provided by Quality Books, Inc.)

Ficalora, Mary T.
Choosing Honor: an American woman's search for God, family and country in an age of corruption / by Mary T. Ficalora.
p. cm.
Includes bibliographical references and index.

1. Social values—United States. 2. United States—Moral conditions. 3. United States—Religion. 4. United States—Social conditions. 5. United States—Economic conditions. 6. Money—United States—Miscellanea. I. Title.

HN90.M6F53 2008 306'.0973
QBI07-600290

First published in hardcover in 2008
Revised softcover edition 2015

Mary Lou Ficalora 1929–1998

To my mother, Mary; she loved
her five children unconditionally
and lived a life dedicated to learning.
She never wavered in her devotion
to the teachings of Jesus Christ
and in her adherence to the
Roman Catholic faith.

Foreword:

Ancora Imparo: I am still learning. Virginia Crane, my editor, gave me a bracelet engraved with those words when *Choosing Honor* was first published in 2008. I wear it everyday. Learning is painful. To claim full understanding of the Mysteries is hubris. I don't. Pain is a constant when realizing what I call the Absolute paths in this book. Terror and war are constant in our existence; they are the easier realizations of the Absolutes, sad to say. The truth of bondage and oppression is all wrapped up in pain and love. For readers who have read the first edition, I do not further discuss pain in this edition. I am also not updating the names of the banks that make up the Money Power running the issuance of currency in the United States and in the World today. The absolute pain the Money Power needs to face has been avoided. The Money Power has been bailed out, reconfigured, renamed, and quantitatively eased on down the road since 2008. Billions of dollars in fines were imposed on economic wrong doers. The wrong doers, banks with complicit government, paid the fines using money the government issued in unison with the banks for the bailouts. Just as the bank might prolong play in the board game *Monopoly*, the bankers and the government dealt money for nothing in order to keep playing. We the people have found it easier to allow the game to continue without indictment or alteration to the rules. The war game plan is still unfolding instead of folding. Terror is still operative.

Yet I have faith in the people, the children of God, Love and the Light, to rise to new levels of consciousness. Love is equal to pain on the Absolute paths; it is up to us to realize love and choose it over pain. War is over if we want it. I believe we, the people, want to end war. To do this we still need to get our money back. Movements like Occupy, Flash Mobs and Thrive, Anonymous, et al., have awakened millions to the need to wake up. We need to continue to pay attention and to act in ways that are the change we want to see in the world. God's Will = Pay Attention. Pope Francis has declared 2015 to be a year of Jubilee. I cannot think of a more auspicious year in which to publish this paperback edition of *Choosing Honor.*

Acknowledgments:

My father, Pete Ficalora, a patriarch in the best sense of the word, authoritarian and loving, unfailing in his integrity and honor, has been a shining example of all that is right with capitalist globalization and conservative thought.

Patric Godderis, a good friend and fellow seeker, gifted me with a copy of Manly P. Hall's *The Secret Teachings of All Ages*. Hall's masterful works have been inspiring my spirit ever since.

Elvira Burton, always a good neighbor, invited me to attend a seminar on kabbalah.

Stephan A. Hoeller, teacher of kabbalah, shared his insights and knowledge of magic, and this "knowing" marked the year of my connecting the dots.

Lucy Solomon, MFT, introduced me to the practice of re-evaluation counseling, a key to recovering our full intelligence.

Saul Ovdat, my real estate agent, took one glance at the library in my home and was inspired to gift me with three more books. In this way I was introduced to the work of Laurence Gardner and to co-authors of *The Messianic Legacy*, Michael Baigent, Richard Leigh and Henry Lincoln.

Ann Gunder, a writer of great common sense, helped me rein in my more radical ideas.

My editor, Virginia Crane, identified points in need of clarification and held me to the task of simplifying and formatting for easier understanding.

Finally, a chance meeting with Victor di Suvero in an art gallery led to his sharing some of his poems with me. Years later as I prepared the first version of this work for mailing, *Let It In* literally fell out of my bookshelf. To my overwhelming surprise, one poem coincides with what I say in this work. Special thanks to Victor for letting me include it here. The time he dedicated to reading and critiquing the first drafts of this work and the insights, support, and suggestions he made for further research contributed enormously to this book.

Thank you all.

LET IT IN

From *"To the Side of Light,"* a work in progress
by Victor di Suvero

In the shadows for too long, it's time to move.
To move to the side of light. We must
Move so as to have those committed to the dark,
Confronted.

We must say "Enough of taking." We
Must, finally, uncover the reasons for disasters.
We must make our words work for all of us.
We have come too far to let the darkness continue
Of those uprooted, moved out, forced into otherness
Under the pretext of common good.
We must say enough.

It is not a time of scarcity.
The fields produce enough to feed the world
And all those who are kept on starvation's edge
By greed proliferating in the dark
It's time to move.

Let the light in.
It takes courage and desire
To move into the side of light
We thrive when we see the sun.

Not enough to be elegantly self referential,
Not enough to be satisfied with the turning
Of a word for the patting of a back or one's
Own good fortune in a cave on mountain side
Or even in green meadows on splendid
Summer days

Table Of Contents

Introduction

I'm a Mother

There can be no life without blood and pain, I know. I'm a mother. Chrissie Hynde sings words to that effect in her song "I'm a Mother" on the Pretenders' *Last of the Independents* album.[1] There is a primal scream in the reality of these words. I know; I'm a mother too. You know; you experienced birth.

Birth, death, blood, pain, sickness, and other people's actions are aspects of life we don't have full control over. They force us to deal with honor. Honor is standing for the good of all in the face of forces we cannot control. In the face of pain, you can choose to lash out and cause everyone else pain too. You can build a wall of apathy and isolate, allowing the pain to fester and oppress you. Or, you can choose to work through your pain, discharge it by crying, and heal. The latter is the honorable way to deal with pain.

Honor then demands that you act to ensure that others do not suffer the same pain in the same way. You act so that others will have help dealing with similar pain. Honor, standing for the good of all, makes the world as one a possibility.

This book is intended to help you find your place of honor. This book is intended to inspire you to take part in realizing one world that operates for the good of all.

My content editor, Virginia Crane, calls me an autodidact. This was a new word for me. Sounds like some kind of addict. This could be oversensitivity on my part, as I do have addictive tendencies. My mantra as a young adult was that I would try anything once. When it came to drugs, my caveat was that I wouldn't use needles. Good caveat; it probably saved my life. Drugs were pervasive in my youth, but they were not my addiction. I am addicted to learning. An autodidact, Virginia let me know, is a person who is self-educated. As far as the content of this book goes, she is absolutely right. I wasn't pursuing a degree when I learned this information. I was seeking answers to my own questions about life. What I have found and share in this book does not come from my conventional education. What I write in this book is also not conventional wisdom.

A lot of what I write contradicts the very basic things most of us have been taught about our religions, our families, and the United States of America. For some people, the information I share will threaten their deepest held beliefs. For me, what I know and share in this book strengthens belief. Understanding what I write clarifies truth from trapping. In the interest of readability, I have blended information. At the same time, I include endnotes and a bibliography for you to check my facts and find out more for yourself.

My formal education is in film and television production. I have a bachelor's degree from Arizona State University and a producing fellow certificate from the American Film Institute. I spent years in television production, working my way up from grip to production manager and producer. Television and film production is a wonderful art form. One engineer early in my career said to me, "The day you stop learning in this business is the day you need to get out." I took that advice to heart and upped it to my philosophy, "The day you stop learning in life is the day you start to die."

After my children were born, my real education began. I left the entertainment business for a new way of life. I also returned to seeking answers to the many spiritual questions I had from my devout Roman Catholic youth. I began working in the education field. I've taught preschool, elementary, and high school students. For over eight years, I have also coordinated, produced, and attended continuing education courses for psychologists. A number of psychologists who are regular attendees of these courses like to joke that I probably know more about personality disorders, mental health issues, and treatments than they do. I do know that a PhD does not give you common sense.

This book comes from my common sense. That being the case, according to Leonardo da Vinci, this book comes from my soul. He wrote, "The soul apparently resides in the seat of judgment, and the judgment apparently resides in the place where all the senses meet, which is called common sense." My soul is crying out.

I was born in 1960 in San Jose, California. The spirit of the peace movement, the women's liberation movement, civil rights, sex, drugs, and rock 'n' roll heavily influence my judgment. I am also the daughter of an IBM engineer. My family spent most of the 1960s and early '70s living in South America and Italy. Globalization—who and what the United States says it is versus who and what it is from an overseas perspective—has also heavily influenced my judgment. The reality that we are currently living in an Age of Corruption has heavily influenced my judgment.

We the People of the United States need a Messiah. Neil Young, a very influential singer and songwriter in my life and in countless others' lives in the 1960-70 era, reflects this need in his 2006 song "Looking for a Leader."

The thing is, Messiahs get assassinated. There will be no one leader, no one Messiah for us. The only ones who are going to end the corruption, despair, apathy, isolation, and violence in our world today are you and me. Regular people like you and me have to step up and realize what is known as Messianic consciousness if the world is going to change. The way we work on the inside has to change. No leader is going to emerge and save us all. Each and every one of us has to become a Messiah. We have to save ourselves. No one is going to come and save us.

The good news is we have all the knowledge and power to do the job. We even have a nation, the United States of America, founded on principles that will enable us to do the job. All we have to do is set what is currently upside down in our nation's principles right side up again.

What I've found to be upside down or in need of attention is in this book. The same things will reflect in your life in ways different from they have in mine. But you will find things to be equally upside down and in need of attention in your life.

The way to being a Messiah is through adherence to a list of Absolutes that I include in this book. These Absolutes do not vary. They are not laws; like gravity, they just are. Adherence to them holds the promise of the power to make miracles happen.

Each of us must discover his or her own way to realizing the miraculous power at work in our lives. My hope is that reading this book will inspire you to pay attention and seek ways to raise yourself to Messianic consciousness. In turn, you will inspire others to do the same and someday the world will be one with the Absolutes.

Someday, we will all be Messiahs with the power to create miracles.

CHAPTER 1
Finding And Protecting God

What a Long Strange Trip It's Been

> *"Sometimes the light's all shining on me_*
> *Other times I can barely see_*
> *Lately it occurs to me_*
> *What a long strange trip it's been."*[3]

In full glare of the light, it is revealed to me that as a citizen of the United States I was born to be president, my own king, a Messiah. All citizens born in the United States wear this mantle. The United States is a nation founded on the idea that we do not need a king to dictate God's will for us. We do not need a Messiah to follow.

We the People with our own free will and inalienable rights can interpret God's will for ourselves. The United States is one nation under God, not under a king or a Messiah – God. We the People are the kings and Messiahs who hold the responsibility for interpreting what God's will is. We the People are responsible for realizing God's kingdom. A lot of religious conditioning obscures this reality. We the People tend to isolate and suppress our own power or to congregate in groups that relegate our Messianic power to religious and political authority. We the People find it easier to wait for a Messiah than to stand upright and strong and take the lead for ourselves. Most of us can barely see our own power.

Music has been huge in helping me see who I am. Music helps me see the power I wield. Music helps me maintain balance and stand upright and be strong. Music pulls me into communion with other people. Music, all music, is a key to our connection to each other. This key is far more than background for a good party and inspiration for horny activity. Music is a manifestation of how the universe actually works.

All living beings are instruments in the symphony of the universe. We are all connected by frequencies.[4] The ancient mystery teachings have a saying: "As it is above, so it is below." Your personal harmony or personal discord directly contributes to the peace or conflict in the entire sphere of creation. The force at work in your personal reality is a reflection of the force at work in our society. The force at work in our society reflects the force at work in our nation. The force at work in our nation reflects the force at work in our global arena. The force at work in our global arena reflects the force at work in the universe as a whole. This force works from the top down; this force works from the bottom up; the force is constant and ever-changing.

We are personally connected to this force. You have a direct impact on the quality of this force's creations. In Western religion, this force is called the Light. Music is a human reflection of the Light. The Light binds us all together with everything in the universe. When all of mankind pays attention to the Light and honors the workings of the Light above all else, the world will be as one. Mankind will have manifested the promised kingdom of God. This is a profound reality, a reality that humanity as a whole has yet to grasp, has yet to realize.

I am Mary, daughter of Mary and granddaughter of Mary. My understanding of the Light took form through my experience as a mother Mary. I was raised in a practicing Roman Catholic family. My parents lived in honor of their unwavering faith. Ten years of my formal education came in Roman Catholic schools. I respected my parents. I respected the teachings, but I was a rebel. I rejected martyrdom, especially the subtle martyrdom women are expected to practice by taking second place to men and the needs of their children. I rejected the mystery of the mysteries. I "knew" the answers to the teachings were in our power to "know." I experienced profound altered consciousness moments in religious ceremony. Yet, I wasn't devoted to the Church and Church law. I have tremendous respect for priests, nuns, monks, and deacons, anyone who devotes himself to his faith. I am sure they are all paying attention to the Light. Yet, my personal spiritual experience was never fully reflected in my religion's settings.

I identify much more closely with the women described in *Women Who Run with the Wolves* by Clarissa Pinkola Estes, PhD.[5] The women in this book live with the "knowing" as a constant companion. Estes' work is a historical documentation of the existence of women with this awareness. She names these women "Wild Women." To my disappointment, Estes did not define what the Wild

Woman experience is. I picked up the book looking for a reflection of myself. I finished the book "knowing" that I understood the "knowing" a lot better than Estes seemed to. For me, being labeled a Wild Woman runs a close second to being called Crazy Mary. What is wild, what is crazy is the "knowing." The "knowing" keeps me free of fear and strong in the face of difficulty.

Jesus Christ taught that the "knowing" is the key to the force of creation. Jesus tells Peter the "knowing" is the "rock" his Church is to be founded upon.[6] This "knowing" is our channeling of the Light. The "knowing" is in every word we speak or do not speak and in every action we take or do not take. Our speech and actions reflect the power of creation and affect the realm without words. Our words and actions do not control this realm. Our words and actions are mere reflections that join forces with the reflections created by the rest of creation and affect creation. All creation channels this power without fully controlling it and manifests the reality we perceive. Our perception of how our power combines with the power of the universe and our perception of how we affect creation and creation affects us constitute the "knowing." The "knowing" powers our "free will."

Religious authorities dictate that this same "knowing" is how we perceive God's will. Ideas about free will and interpreting God's will get bogged down in material concerns and emotional attachments. We need to understand what exactly "will" is.

I've studied comparative religion as well as obscure and mainstream esoteric writings, and I have found that God's will is energy. This energy, the Light, is the creative force of the Universe. This energy is ever-changing and is constantly bringing our existence into form. The positioning of all matter in the Universe, according to the prophecy of ages, influences our perception of this energy. We are matter. Our "will" is our ability to alter our positioning in the Universe by receiving and reflecting the creative force. Our will maintains, redirects, and/or disrupts this force's balance.

Thus, the spiritual mandate of adherence to God's will is to PAY ATTENTION! The creative force of the universe is constant. The creative force of the universe is harmonious, ever-changing and without end. Tapping into this force gives us an intense rush of excitement and a sense of joyous celebration, of unknown new beginnings.

Pay attention to the balance in the forces of creation as they affect you. Pay attention to all that is not in balance. Pay attention to how the imbalance is affecting us. Pay attention to how the imbalance is affecting the world around us. Pay attention to how others are affecting the balance. Pay attention to how you are affecting the balance. We need to be conscious of our "will" balancing the changes in creation. We need to be conscious of how the "will" of others is affecting the balance of creation.

Recognition of the power of the Light at work enables us to use it to manifest the existence we desire. We can master reflections of the Light. We can create the reality we desire. But the Light is the real power. We can only reflect the Light. We are not the Light. The Light works for all of creation, not just you and me. God's will is at work for the good of all creation.

Our "will" in full harmony with the force of creation unites us with the life force, the power we cannot control. Our "will" in full harmony with God's will unites us with the mystical All. The All is what religions call the one God. Uniting with the one God requires us to raise our levels of consciousness to realize the good of all. We raise our consciousness by paying attention, being present, "knowing" from the signs around us what the good of all is. Each of us has the ability to do this. Our wills are free to either mirror God's will or refract God's will. We choose to act for the good of all or for the good of self. We have free will. We have honor when we choose to act for the good of all.

God's will in Western religion is often called the Light. Some Eastern religions call this Chi. The Light can be manipulated just like rays of light. The Light bends, diffuses, changes in color, dims, and blacks out according to our will. Ultimately, the Light returns to its original trajectory. Light always reconfigures to a rainbow, infinitely moving, constant in force. God's will always reconfigures. Regardless of the changes wrought by our will, the Light always returns to its form at the point of creation. The infinite variation of our choices alters the quality of the Light's creations, but we never alter its creative energy. Like gravity, God's will is an energy that has no beginning or end; it just is.

What I have said here is consistent with the belief systems of most Eastern and Western religions. What conflict with my vision of God and the Universe are religious dictates that attempt to define the experience of interfacing with God's will. These dictates are man-made and often rigid in their definition. They honor messiahs of the past; they even make some of them God.

Each messiah, teacher, king, saint, rabbi, and pope who has perceived and shared the interface with God's will with humanity is different. Their experiences are not. They all essentially reflect the same energy, the same experience, the same force of creation. What differ are the dictates that guide followers to the Light according to each teacher's experience, culture, and customs. The Light at work, the raising of our consciousness to become one with the Light for the good of all, does not differ. The dictates are man-made prescriptions for behavior and ceremony designed to enable interfacing with the Light, God's will.

Religious dictates were created to unite people with the Light. Sadly, many of these dictates have evolved into religious laws that block the working of the Light rather than enable it to unite us. Religious law has inspired religious superiority and exclusiveness and interferes with humanity achieving oneness with the universe.

Humanity as a whole just wants decent food, shelter, and clothing. We want to live in peace to pursue happiness. We all know that a life in which our needs are met, a life filled with unconditional love, is the ideal. Humanists and atheists can find no fault with operating for the good of all any more than the religious can. Hinduism, Buddhism, Judaism, Christianity, Islam, and the less well-known religions are all efforts to realize life in ideal form. In spite of universal agreement on what the ideal is, greed and the desire to control the supply of food, shelter, and clothing have twisted the ideal away from the good of all over and over again.

Every war ever waged has claimed higher cause. War for a higher cause that will realize a common good is nothing but a lie. The only higher cause worthy of being called a higher cause is harmony. It's a travesty that blood has been shed and is still being shed over invented boundaries in religion and ideology.

Followers of Islam, Judaism, and Christianity all claim to be children of the same

God. The current fighting in the Middle East is based on false differences that we've been conditioned to believe are truths. Buddhists and Hindus are relegated to the ranks of unbelievers in Western "one God" circles. They are not one with the belief held by Judeo-Christian "chosen ones." These "chosen ones" in turn kill each other over interpretations of God's will that dictate who is going to control the material world. These "one God" believers are relegated to the ranks of unbelievers in Eastern religions. Differentiations between followers of the Light, believers in the one God, and those who seek nirvana and a supreme power are false differentiations.

False differentiations are an integral part of our modern spirituality. These differentiations are based on psychological conditioning that is rooted in practices that have lost their original intent. This kind of conditioning is beautifully demonstrated in the story about a black cat that makes a pest of itself during meditation hour in an ashram in India. The master directs that the cat be tied to a post in the courtyard during meditation to stop the distraction. Years pass, the master dies, and the tying up of the cat becomes part of daily ritual. When the cat is found dead of old age one morning, the community members panic over how and where they will find a replacement in time for the meditation hour. They'd been conditioned to believe the cat tied to the post in the courtyard is essential to their spiritual practice.[7]

Many religious leaders and communities cling to boundaries of theological thought in the same way. Just as the black cat was not essential to meditation, the differences between Buddhism, Hinduism, Islam, Christianity, Judaism, and countless other faiths are not essential to those faiths. Yet conditioning is so rigid that some believers will kill before they will acknowledge that their faith is equal to another faith. Free thinking has been oppressed. To kill to protect "God's law" defeats "God." Killing extinguishes a reflection of God. To reject another human being for spiritual reasons is incongruous to the working of the Light. We cannot find the Light by killing or rejecting our fellow reflectors of it. The Light is a harmonious unconditional constant.

Authorities use superiority of faith and ideologies to justify war and protect their control of material wealth. Both superiority and war are an abomination of the Light.

The Light has no attachment to what it creates. One creation is as sacred as any other creation. Attachment to creation creates an emotional value that inspires false superiority. To be one with the Light means we lose all attachment to material creation. Attachment is hubris. Attachment inspires fighting to control creation; fighting blocks creation. War blocks the Light.

War is based on the tying up of black cats. These black cats are distractions. We humans have been conditioned to pay attention to distractions from a very young age. Paying attention to the actual energy at work in our lives is not easy.

My young adult years were riddled with drug use and sexual promiscuity. It was the late 1970s and early '80s; drugs were readily available. Sexuality was celebrated. Church law was in my opinion up to interpretation, and interpretation can contradict itself. I concluded very early in life that no authority—religious, social, or political—would ever tell me if I was one with the Light or not. I alone "knew." I "knew" the Church was not telling all. I "knew" that the mystery of the mysteries could be solved, but answers were not readily available. What happened to the dawning of the age of Aquarius? What happened to the peace movement? Answers were not readily available.

My personal attempt to tackle these questions was often ridiculed by my peers. I was told and I accepted that religion is the "opiate of the masses." Organized religion was and is designed to maintain ignorance and manipulate us into subjugation to authority. My forays into seeking insights and questions regarding peace and the validity of US foreign policy were met with the unending litany of "So what are you going to do? Get yourself shot?" I studied mass communication, worked in television production, and entered film school. I am ashamed to admit it was easier to smoke pot, dance my heart out to great music, and play with making music videos than to tackle the "authorities." Eventually, raising children became more important than addressing the state of the world.

I have three children: Max, twenty-five; Charlotte, twenty-two; and Mia, thirteen. Becoming a mother is how the full impact of what it means to live a life of honor took form for me. Marriage should have done this; that's what the vows were all about. For me, the realization of why the vow to honor is in the marriage vows came via the realization of dishonor. Sordid personal details aside, by the early 1990s I was a full-time mother and my mind returned to seeking answers to the mysteries.

The teaching "Seek and you shall find" took root in my soul, and the Philosophical Research Society in Los Angeles was just across the park from where I lived. I attended PRS services, bought books from its bookstore, and took many of the society's esoteric classes. In all, I've spent more than sixteen years studying spiritual knowledge.

Spiritual knowledge just is. Reality requires us to pay attention to material knowledge if we want to survive. Spiritual knowledge is reflected in material knowledge. Yet, beyond affecting the way we treat others, spiritual knowledge rarely crosses over into our material consciousness. Or so I thought. Alarm bells went off in my head when President George W. Bush started talking about warring against evil in his buildup to invading Iraq in 2003. You cannot war against evil. To war against evil is to war against good. They are both the force of creation. Good and evil are different frequencies on the Light's spectrum. They are both the Light.

You can only harmonize them to the Light. You cannot kill evil or good.

The move to brand the Islamic religion as evil is old history. Islam is no more evil than Christianity is. "Might makes right" warring between Christian and Islamic zealots in the holy lands is a dead end. "Might makes right" is a dead end. To kill to prove you are one with God's will is a travesty of both religions. So much killing has happened in God's name over the centuries, it's a wonder anyone still believes in God.

Religious fervor is history's primary "terror tool" used to motivate a people to war. War is a manipulation of human will. War destroys the All. Honor is our only defense. Our power as individuals to know the Light and refuse to dishonor it is how the mystical All takes form. The very existence of God, our families, and the United States depends on our honor.

Modeling how to live a life of honor is a parent's job. I take the "teach your children well"[8] sentiment expressed in song during my youth very seriously. My two oldest children spent their childhoods answering the question, "What are you fighting for?" I was a thorn in their sides during their Power

Ranger and Pokemon phases. Role-playing the characters from these shows was their favorite pastime.

"What are you fighting for?" I would ask.

"We're fighting the bad guys," they'd answer.

"How do you know they're bad guys?"

"They want to take over the world."

"So what?"

I drove them nuts with my insistence that stopping a bad guy from taking over the world was not a good enough answer. We needed to know why the bad guys wanted to take over the world. What was their motivation? Would the world be a better place if these bad guys did take it over? If the toy company or the television show didn't supply the answers, then we discussed ideals and what was worth fighting for.

Max always ended up fighting to be his own boss. My older daughter, Charlotte, usually fought to keep sole possession of her toys. I approved both thought processes. My approval opened up the next range of ethical questioning. "As your own boss, are there any rules?" "How do you treat others?" "The things you are fighting to keep, do you have a right to them?" "Are they yours to keep?"

"Does somebody else need them?" "Do you need them as much as someone else?"

To me, constant questioning of our motivations and the motivations of the authorities in our lives is essential to the mastery of our existence. Paying attention requires constant questioning and listening.

Max and Charlotte taught me as much as I taught them. Clear guidelines for defining a "bad" guy are important to me. Defining "bad guys" became equally important to my children. Max, for example, startled me when he pointed out that Darth Vader actually did bring balance to the force. I'd missed this very crucial understanding of the Star Wars story.

For those of you who do not know the storyline, Darth Vader betrayed his "masters," the Jedi Knights, protectors of the Force. Darth Vader killed children and selfishly wielded his power to harness the Force for personal desire and authoritarian control over the empire. He was a brutal dictator who betrayed teachers who had trained him as the possible Jedi of prophesy that was going to bring balance to the force.

I missed the understanding that, in the end, Darth Vader did fulfill the prophecy.

Darth returned to the Light. Darth killed his evil master to protect his son, Luke. Luke was a Jedi that operated in full balance. Luke used the Light as needed. Luke didn't differentiate between the powers of the dark and the powers of the Light. Wielding the power of the force is all about balance. Max was paying better attention than I was.

"Bad" guys are not always who or what we think they are. From England's perspective back in 1776, "bad" guys founded the United States of America. The Declaration of Independence declares that knowledge of what is spiritually right outweighs what is ruled right by authorities in the material world. Every man who signed that document knew he was risking his life. Signing was a point of honor.

What do I tell my children our great nation is fighting for today in our "War on Terror"? My children know the simplistic story behind the Iraq war. Our nation is fighting evil perpetrated by people who are jealous of us. They know this story is a joke in the face of the spiritual knowledge I have taught them. When a jealous person hits you, it's not OK to hit back. That would be fighting evil with evil. We cannot "win" a war against evil. Evil can only be harmonized, changed to good, raised to the higher power of good. Our government is failing to own the essential truth that evil is not separate from us. Whenever evil has been allowed to manifest in violence in humanity, there is something very wrong within the workings of all the participants in the conflict: evil begets evil, good begets good.

M. Scott Peck tackled the nature of evil in *People of the Lie.*[9] People of the Lie say their motivation is one thing when in fact it is something else. Peck, a military psychiatrist during the Vietnam War, was the chairman of a 1972 committee of three psychiatrists appointed by the army surgeon general to find the root causes of atrocities committed by our troops against civilians, in particular the My Lai massacre. Their task was to recommend actions to ensure our troops didn't commit such acts again. The committee proposed a research plan that the army general staff rejected because the plan would not be able to be kept secret and might prove embarrassing to the administration. The proposal addressed the compartmentalization of responsibility. The morality of the war, for example, was not the military-industrial complex's department. Yet, the munitions industry, motivated by profits, was playing a large role in military policy. Our soldiers carried out this policy and found themselves fighting for the freedom of a people who did not want us there.

Peck's committee's recommendations were not followed up on. Not facing our collective responsibility, not facing our own failure to control our part in harnessing power, is dishonor. In light of our authorities' dishonorable decision to not act on Peck's findings, Peck predicted a repeat of the same mistakes in twenty years. Iraq, Abu Ghraib, and the CIA torture scandals prove Peck a prophet.

Prophecy is the act of bringing the "knowing" into words. What was going to embarrass the American people was the fact that we supported a war without knowing what we were fighting for. We sent troops to kill without knowing why they were killing. The public position taken by the administration was that we were fighting the spread of Communism. Anyone who has studied Political Theory 101 knows that Communism itself is not evil. The evil is in the means used by authorities to implement the ideal. This is true for capitalism and any other "ism."

Peck defined evil as action taken by people who lie about the reasons for their action. We are all People of the Lie. We all say our families love each other, yet we all have unloving patterns in our families. This level of being one of the People of the Lie is personal.

The Vietnam War made us all People of the Lie on a national scale, as does the war in Iraq. President George W. Bush lied about weapons of mass destruction in Iraq. The war in Iraq is being waged for a lie. We are the People of the Lie as long as our military stays in control of Iraq. The delay in our troop withdrawal has to do with the real reason we are there: control of Iraqi oil and how it is going to be sold. Every other reason for our military presence in Iraq is secondary. Honor demands that we be embarrassed. Honor demands that we own our own evil. We are all imperfect. Owning the imperfection allows for the pursuit of happiness.

"The American dream," says Gabriele Muccino, the director of the film *Pursuit of Happyness*, "that hope, that possibility of becoming what you desire, is close to God. That's what godliness is."[10] To be part of one nation under God means we seek to be godly.

I tell my children that We the People are fighting evil in the "War on Terror." We the People are fighting the greatest evil on earth. That evil is ignorance. We the People do not know that the evil we are fighting is within ourselves. Terror comes from our own lack of godliness.

We the People do not know that we are the Messiahs responsible for setting our one nation to right. Our perceptions of truth vary. Our material realities vary. The ways we find harmony with our loved ones vary. Our "black cats" vary. The essential truth remains the same. We the People wear the mantle of Messiah in the United States; it comes with being citizens of one nation under God. We are all interconnected parts of the whole that is our nation under God. It is our responsibility to "know." It is up to you and me to rise above terror. The solution is within us. Peace can only exist if we harmonize the forces of conflict in our lives. Freedom is only possible if we realize it. This war is literally a war for control of your heart and mind. We the People have to "know." We the People have to actually be who we say and think we are.

CHAPTER 2
The Absolutes

For What It's Worth

In 1967, Stephen Stills sang about something happening; he called our attention to gunshots ringing out and the realization that who was right and who was wrong wasn't clear. He named this song, "For What It's Worth," a title that conveys hope in the face of powerlessness.[11] His lyrics cry out for us to pay attention to authoritarian forces that strike fear in us when we dare to speak out against them. This is 2007; there is a new generation and a new conflict, but the forces at work remain the same. The need for everyone to look at "what's going down" is the same today as it was when Stills first sang, "For What It's Worth."

Most of our citizens do not know what our military is fighting for in Iraq any more than we knew what was being fought for in Vietnam. We rally to the rants of radio jocks demanding unquestioning public support for the cause. Support is given despite evidence that leaders have lied to us. We do not really know why we were lied to. We do not know what is really going on, but we brand anyone who dissents unpatriotic. Dissent, we are told, undermines the morale of the brave men and women who are sacrificing their lives for what we do not know. National secrecy and unquestioning support for secrets is the norm. The average citizen has no idea what the United States government is doing around the world and why. I know this is true because I am one of these average citizens. I have only just begun to start paying attention.

The death of John F. Kennedy Jr. shocked me out of my comfort with ignorance. I had subscribed to his *George* magazine as soon as I'd read the first issue. A lot of my hopes for the United States' future were pinned on John F. Kennedy Jr. No one else on the public stage glowed of potential greatness and trustworthiness.

Then came the 2000 presidential election and the inconsistency between exit polls and election results. I "knew" all was not right in the workings of the United States. I started reading beyond the surface stories found in mainstream headline news.

During the 2004 presidential election, I worked long hours writing letters to editors around the country. I was driven to respond to ideas and statements made by the Swift Boat veterans and religious "right" thinkers. Hundreds of e-mails came and went from my computer. The Swift Boat veterans' attack on John Kerry's support for ending the war struck me as either a sign that our president had no control over his supporters or proof that our president had no honor.

A few of my favorite friends were devoted to the Bush administration. Part of my family supported Bush. The religious core that held them loyal to the administration scared me a few times. But I held firm with my campaign to hold to the truth. In the Vietnam era, Kerry, a decorated veteran, earned the right to stand up and ask the question, "How do you ask a man to be the last to die for a mistake?"

He asked a valid question. Our nation did make a mistake by going to Vietnam. The parallels between Vietnam and Iraq were, to me, screamingly obvious. In 2004, my letters questioned the morality of our foreign relations in Iraq, the Abu Ghraib torture revelations, and the scare tactics used in Bush campaign commercials.

The Republican campaign was about fear. Commercials showed wolves running in the woods that were going to get us if we let Kerry lead us. Others showed atomic bombs that were going to go off in our cities if we let Kerry win. This scaremongering, to me, was terrorism. If our fight was righteous, why did our citizens have to be scared into fighting? Why did going to war in Iraq require a lie? Why did we have to resort to torture? Why were we not hearing positive messages from a position of strength based on a list of facts that cast obvious Light on the work that needs to be done?

I didn't perceive honesty from either the Republicans or the Democrats in the 2004 presidential election. Kerry did not defend his Vietnam stance nor did he take an equally brave stance regarding Iraq. Kerry stood down. Valor was a thing of his past. Bush was a fear monger. Neither candidate entered into honest exploration of the facts, the history, and the events that led us to war in Iraq. I perceived fear dominating everyone. Honor was not evident.

Honor is everything when it comes to wielding Messianic power. The power of kings in western tradition is derived from Messianic teachings. All leaders, all public figures are wielding Messianic power. Honorable working of Messianic power is defined by sayings such as "All for one, and one for all." Traditional Messianic power works by the people lending all their power to the king (the Messiah) and in return the king dedicates all the power he wields for the good of all. The king must stand for honor if the people are to prosper. Honor is standing for the good of all in situations of powerlessness. A king without honor is a despot. Despotism is a mandate for revolution in the United States of America.

You and I are "We the People." We the People of the United States of America are sovereign. That means we hold the power of king in our nation. We the People are the one and the all. President John F. Kennedy's famous line from his inaugural speech, "Ask not what your country can do for you—ask what you can do for your country," tapped into the Messianic power at work in the United States of America. We the People are the kings of the United States, thus We the People must be ever-vigilant that we give back as much as we take. We the People must be ever-vigilant in how our power is being wielded. We the People have to stand for honor in the face of forces we cannot control.

Messianic teachings are not religion. Messianic teachings are not "church," as in separation of church and state. Both church and state interpret the Messianic teachings. Church interpretations are emotion based and driven by faith and prophesy. The church honors the miraculous mysteries of life. State interpretations are based on rational facts. The state honors justice in the face of humanity's imperfections. Justice is not faith based. Justice does not require church. Justice is not well served by emotions, faith, and prophetic predictions. Thus, We the People have the separation of church and state.

For Christians, Messianic teachings are what James Robison, a popular Christian leader in the United States today, calls the Absolutes in *The Absolutes, Freedom's Only Hope*. Robison, like most religious leaders, defines the Absolutes by inference[12] made from studying Jesus Christ's life and the dictates of the Bible.

Using Christ's life and the Bible as a model for establishing the Absolutes is an ancient practice. The problem is that the Bible contradicts itself. On the one hand Jesus Christ tells us that God is the Light. God is unconditional love. On the other hand there is the Creator God, the God author Richard Dawkins in *The God Delusion* says is:

> arguably the most unpleasant character in all fiction: jealous and proud of it; a petty, unjust, unforgiving control-freak; a vindictive, bloodthirsty ethnic cleanser; a misogynistic, homophobic, racist, infanticidal, genocidal, filicidal, pestilential, megalomaniacal, sadomasochistic, capriciously malevolent bully.[13]

The Creator God has no love to spare for the human race. My early religious training was marked by frustration over the fact that religious law and universal truths—what I now call, thanks to Robison, the Absolutes—are defined by inference gleaned from this inconsistent source.

I now believe the contradictions in the Bible exist because the Bible is actually the outcome of tens, if not hundreds, of thousands of years of "playing telephone" with kabbalah, an ancient body of esoteric writings. Kabbalah is also known as the Tree of Life teachings, also known as the Messianic teachings.

I grew up believing in Jesus Christ as "the Messiah" of prophesy. No one ever taught me that the original teachings that made him a Messiah also teach that we are all mandated to follow the same paths and become Messiahs ourselves. I was surprised to find out that kabbalist teaching is that the "end of days," the prophesied time we will enter the kingdom of God, will be when all of mankind achieves Messianic consciousness. Mastering kabbalah, mastering the Absolutes, is how you attain Messianic consciousness.

Christians are not taught that kabbalah is where you find the teachings that define a Messiah. Christians are not taught that kabbalah is what Christ based his work on. Christians are not taught that the Book of Revelations in the New Testament is a reflection of kabbalist teaching. Christians are not taught that making laws based on kabbalist teachings counters kabbalist teachings.

You cannot make definitive law based upon the forces that balance the Light without ensnaring yourself in violation of these forces at the same time. The forces of balance, the Absolutes, can only be recognized and honored. Honor cannot be enforced. Recognition cannot be legislated without judging. The Absolutes just are; they are not good or evil. As Christ taught, judging has to be left to the Light.[14] Knowledge and understanding of the Absolutes do not qualify us to judge others. The force of creation always rights itself. The balance of the Light is as inevitable as gravity.

To clarify what the Absolutes are, I've returned to the source. The Tree of Life, kabbalah, is a diagram. This diagram, illustrated here, is a map of paths through which we connect to the Light. I've focused on the ten primary paths found on the Tree. These paths, the circles in the diagram, are called Sephiroths. These are "hub" paths that dictate the workings of all the other paths. I've stripped these primary paths down to their essential meanings. I start at the tenth Sephiroth, the path at the bottom of the tree, and work my way up to the first Sephiroth at the top of the tree.

Each of these Absolutes is a point of honor. If all of humanity lives in honor of these Absolutes at all times, there is no need

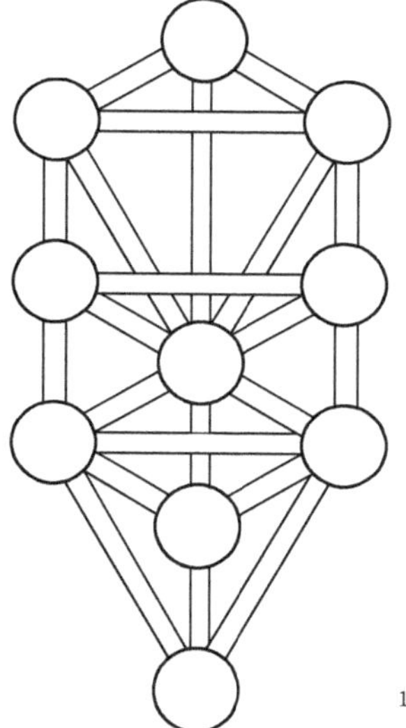

[15]

for law, government, or authority. Humanity honoring these Absolutes makes the existence of God, Family, and the United States possible. Honoring these Absolutes is how you make miracles happen.

1) ALL LIFE REFLECTS THE LIGHT

The Light is the power of creation. All life reflects the Light. The Light we reflect affects our existence. The Light we reflect comes back to affect us. Thus, all life must be honored as we would honor ourselves.

2) WE ALL HAVE EQUAL POWER

All human beings are autonomous and

independent reflectors of the Light. Some of us seem to master reflecting the Light, paying attention, "knowing," faster, more clearly than others. But no human has any greater ability than any other to affect existence by reflecting the Light. All of us have the potential to achieve Messianic consciousness.

3) UNITING MAGNIFIES OUR POWER

Combining our reflections of the Light with the reflections of others on the same "frequency" exponentially increases the power of that frequency to affect our existence. Families are more powerful than individual family members. Communities are more powerful than families. States are more powerful than communities. Nations are more powerful than states, and so on.

4) WE ALL HAVE A PURPOSE

Being one with the Light is to further the work of Creation. We must find our purpose, the work we seem born to do. Such work maintains the balance of the Light because we become one with the force of Creation.

5) CHANGE IS CONSTANT

Ascendance requires nonattachment.

In the workings of the Light, change is a constant. The important art of life is not to stand in the way of change and right things happening.

6) WHAT WE CREATE IS SACRED

The force of Creation is sacred. We interface with the creative force and thus have the power to create. We are reflections of God, the Light, the force of Creation. What the Light creates is sacred. Everything we create is sacred too.

7) LOVE ALL

To be in full interface with the Light is to love everyone we meet. To love another is to love one's self. This Absolute is not sexual. It is about unconditional love. Love is the All; it is us. The Light is Love. Love is the force of creation. Thus, all of us are reflections of the rest of us. We are all good.

8) BIRTH AND DEATH ARE THE SAME THING

As painful as it is to deal with in the moment of giving up, there is new life with every death. There also is death with every birth. In the All there is grief at birth that matches our grief at death. In the All there is an intense joy of reception at death that matches the joy of reception at birth.

9) ALL THAT WE ASK FOR IS GIVEN TO US

Everything we ask for materializes. If we are in tune with the "knowing," we find that we "never want." Our perception of time keeps us from being fully aware of this truth. Neglecting to focus on what we need versus what we want results in our perception of needs not being met. Changing our minds, losing direction, and not knowing what we want contribute to our perception or lack of perception of this Absolute.

10) ALL OF CREATION IS ONE CREATION

All of creation is one connected whole powered by the Light. The same frequencies of attraction hold all and bring all of creation into form.

To me, this list of Absolutes is secular. To honor them, you are not required to adhere to a religion. At the same time, these Absolutes parallel in one way or another most of the teachings found in mankind's major religions.

Kabbalists believe the Tree of Life teachings come from the Creator God. Some say they were given to the sons of Adam. Some say they were given to Moses along with the Ten Commandments. Historically, knowledge of the Tree's teachings and insight into the source of the knowledge has been the domain of priest kings. Time lines that track the ruling years of these priest kings go back hundreds of thousands of years and merge into Christian tradition in which popes ordained kings.[16]

Achieving Messianic consciousness was an integral part of the early Christian Gnostic movement. Gnostic means knowing. The Gnostics placed the "knowing" above all else in the practice of Christianity. Their stance caused serious problems in the formation of a Church hierarchy in the first few hundred years of the Christian faith. Specific documentation of Gnostic policies or a time line of events that led to their demise is hard to find. I like to think that, like early Americans, the Gnostics did not believe they needed a "king" to dictate how the Absolutes were to be honored.

Gnostics were branded heretics and excommunicated from the Church. Their scriptures, including the Gospel of Thomas, were destroyed. Copies of these documents were rediscovered in 1946 in a place called Nag Hammadi in Egypt. The complete collection, known as the Nag Hammadi Library, had been safely buried for over fifteen hundred years.

My father, a devout Roman Catholic, has an instant fear response to the mention of Gnostic belief. Gnostic interpretations of the Absolutes invite accusations of heresy and excommunication to this day.

I do not think everyone needs to study kabbalah. I do think everyone needs to be aware of all that is at the root of the religion they practice. Kabbalah is, I believe, THE root of all of mankind's major religions, Eastern and Western. There are infinite scriptural parallels and beliefs to support my claim. To me, symbolism alone makes source differentials a moot point.

This symbolic revelation came to me when I played with drawing the Tree of Life in four-dimensional form as the teachings dictate. I was astounded when I fleshed out a drawing that could represent a diagram of DNA! I have since discovered that I am not the only modern kabbalist to have divined this similarity.[17]

DNA and the Tree of Life diagram reflect each other. In the Tree of Life teachings, ALL is a reflection of the Tree of Life. With DNA, all life is composed of DNA. The paths of the Tree of Life are said to be four dimensional, combining in infinite ways. DNA has four amino acids that combine in infinite ways. The power of the Light travels the Tree in a spiral motion and moves in an infinite combination of frequencies along the paths. DNA's four amino acids string together in an infinite array of combinations along a double-helix spiral to form an infinite number of life forms.

Path of the Serpent on the Tree of Life[18]

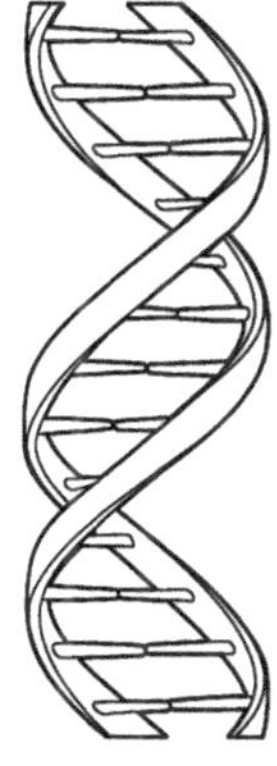

DNA[19]

Even more startling is the parallel imagery that exists between a cross-cut slice of DNA and religious symbols. The rose window pattern found in Cathedrals is the most dramatic. DNA designs can be found on ancient Koran cases.

Cross-cut Slice of DNA[20]

Rose Window

Ancient Koran Case

Sri Yantra (ancient mandala of creation)[21]

This same pattern is reflected in the mandala of Hindu and Buddhist religions. The mandala has always been said to model the cosmic design, the organizational structure of life itself.

The Sri Yantra mandala, the mandala of creation, is of particular interest in relation to the Tree of Life diagram. Work has been done with the lines in the Sri Yantra that reveals a direct correlation to the four dimensional paths of the Tree of Life.[22] I also find it fascinating that if you look closely at the center of the Sri Yantra, you can see a Star of David. This mandala design goes back thousands of years. No one knows its origin.

What all this parallel imagery means is a puzzle. Archeological clues are startling and hard to believe. All priest kings who ruled as the first Messiahs are written to have been "beings from the sky."[23] The "beings from the sky" were considered gods. Translations of the "beings from the sky" stories tell of genetic manipulations and cross-breeding between "beings from the sky" and an earth species.[24] These mind-boggling translations of ancient texts mirror Bible stories. They are so hard to believe that my instinct is to simply reject them. Instead, I take the stance that the Roman Catholic Church has taken: nothing discovered changes the teachings of Jesus Christ.[25] All life is subject to the force of creation. If we are created from a previously existing species, that species is also subject to the Absolutes that dictate the workings of the force of creation.

Jesus Christ modeled a life that honors the Absolutes found on the Tree of Life diagram. Regardless of the source of this diagram, there can be no doubt that honoring the Absolutes is the best way to deal with forces in our lives that we are all connected to and that none of us control.

To me, it is also important to get beyond religious belief and into rational secular thought. The most exciting secular development in the study of Messianic teachings is the work done by world-renowned psychologist, Carl Jung. Jung worked extensively with the Tree of Life paths. He named the paths in the diagram our collective unconscious.[26] Jung named personality types according to the workings of the four layers of each path. Thanks to Jung, mastering God's will, paying attention, is now known as achieving conscious interface with the unconscious. The psychological term for Messianic consciousness is now wholeness. To achieve wholeness is to achieve full attention, an unfettered awareness of the present.

Wholeness requires us to fully integrate honor of the Absolutes into our existence. Jung calls this integrating our "shadow." To be whole is to operate in full honor, full "knowing." This "knowing" is not knowledge of facts. This "knowing" is awareness, a consciousness. To be a Master requires rising above the imperfections of the world that just are in order to realize the power of the creative force at work: the Light that we reflect. "Knowing" is what enables us to divine the good of all. "Knowing" is what enables empathy and compassion, without which we become isolated and powerless.

Feelings of isolation and powerlessness are pervasive in the citizenry of the United States of America today. Through my studies I have come to believe that we isolate ourselves because of our feelings of powerlessness, feelings which are rooted in the disconnect between what we say we consider to be the fundamental values of our existence versus the reality of our existence.

We say we honor each human being and each is entitled to equal rights to life, liberty, and the pursuit of happiness. Yet we live lives of debt-ridden dependence on employment that is always threatening to disappear. "It's business" is a mantra that allows for apathetic disconnection and instills powerlessness. The idea of us as individuals deserving liberty to pursue happiness has become "Get a job."

We are sovereigns without any control over or knowledge of our military's operations. If we observe our foreign military and economic policies in the "War on Terror," we see that the reality is we reserve the right to life, liberty, and the pursuit of happiness to those who support, without question, the US government and its policies. Citizens who protest US policy risk being labeled threats to national security interests or even being thought of as terrorists. People our President deems threats don't even get the rights afforded to Jeffery Dahmer, a murderer who ate his victims. Serial killers and child rapists today have more legal rights and protection in the United States than a citizen accused of being a threat to national security.

The "War on Terror" has the executive branch of the US government reserving the right to torture and hold alleged threats to national security without charges. The executive branch takes this position of extreme authority in total disregard of the fact that the International Court of Justice and the United Nations Security Council has found the United States to be a leading state sponsor of terrorism. High-profile examples of our terrorist operations include actions in Nicaragua during the 1980s, in Chile from 1963-1973, and in Cuba from the 1960s and on through the 1990s.[27] Our mode of operation in the Vietnam War was terrorist based.[28] Military operations designed to "psych" enemies into capitulation are a standard mode of operation. We the People know this, if only subconsciously.

We had a hit television show in the '70s called *The A Team* that played out small-scale terrorist operations every week for our entertainment. A lead character, Mr. T, was loved for his ability to strike terror in the hearts of the enemies his team was hired to scare into capitulation. The US government's disavowal of its terrorist actions, including the policy of betraying our own operatives, was written into this show. The audience seemingly accepted that our government operates in this way.

Vietnam was a war of terror. Iraq is said to be a war on terror. War on terror, war of terror, there is no difference. We the People are supporting an ongoing government policy of terror and simultaneous denial of terror. We are in denial that we are terrorists as we fight terrorists. The US operates a foreign policy in which it is a given that we do not treat others as we would treat ourselves.

To treat others as you would have others treat you is to stand in honor. Treating others as you would have them treat you is the number one mandate in wielding Messianic power. We the People need to pay attention to the power being wielded. We the People need to pay attention to the power we wield. We the people need to regain our honor.

Messianic power is not just something Jesus had. Messianic power is a power we wield in every waking moment of our lives. If we don't pay attention to how we use this power, Christ's interpretations of how to use it are easily turned upside down.

Going to war to further God's will is an example of upside-down interpretation of the Absolutes. The concept of a "love conquers all" that includes the use of military might is an upside-down interpretation of the Absolutes used in the U.S. military today. Michael L. Weinstein and Davin Seay in *With God on Our Side: One Man's War Against an Evangelical Coup in America's Military* detail the growth of evangelism in the US military.[29] This new evangelism employs military might as a way to the work of Jesus.

This kind of upside-down interpretation of the Absolutes leads mankind into subjugation to a "Messiah."

The transition of a Messiah from a follower of the Light who lives as an example to a Messiah who lives as a refractor of the Light is the very essence of what it means to be a Christ versus an anti-Christ. Reflecting the Light as a shining example of the Absolutes versus harnessing the reflections of humanity's Light to gain Absolute power is the difference between living a life of honor and living a life of dishonor.

We have mandated separation of church and state in the United States to protect citizens from despotic leaders who use the Absolutes in upside-down ways. To turn the US military into "soldiers for Christ" is an abomination of everything the United States and Jesus stand for. We the People have not been paying attention.

CHAPTER 3
Money Is Our Magic Wand

Mind Games

Consciousness, paying attention, honor, and setting the United States to right are mind games. John Lennon sang truth in his quest to bring power to the people. He called for us to "Keep on playing those mind games together."[30] The ultimate and and most creative "mind game" we must play is to master the Absolutes in our own lives.

To master the Absolutes is to realize our power to reach Messianic consciousness, and this, funny as it sounds, is the same as realizing our power as "Magicians." Magician, Master, and Messiah are interchangeable terms. All three are names for the mastery of the power to alter our perceptions of reality, manifest our reality, and change our reality.

Knowing that our government needs to be set right causes despair and powerlessness in citizens. If only we could wave a "magic wand" and make it all better. The good news is we can. We do wield a magic wand, and we use it every day of our lives. It's money.

Money is magic. Money is responsible for mankind's state of existence. The creation of money, the value of money, and how money works is Magic that we create and control. President Abraham Lincoln called the people behind the creation of and the workings of money the "Money Power."[31] The Money Power in the world would have us think the power is out of our hands. It's not. The value of money is an illusion we all choose to participate in and support.

We practice Magic every waking moment of our lives. Magic is an ancient name for the Light; it is another name for God's will. The word "magic" derives from magnes, the stone with magnetic properties that came from the island of Magnesia. Today, we call everything with this property a magnet.

Magi, or a magus in the singular, who honor Magic originally were Zoroastrian priests. The story of the baby Jesus includes three Magi visiting his cradle. Magic is intimately related to the story of Jesus Christ. The Magi who visited baby Jesus were called kings; Jesus Christ was called king. Their right to the title has to do with being Messiahs, wielders of Messianic power.

The popular magician is more court jester than king. The entertainer magician is an illusionist who tricks his audience. This practice has been misused. Magicians have come to be viewed with suspicion. Jesus Christ, the Messiah of Christianity, was no different in this sense. In his lifetime Jesus was accused of being a charlatan, a master of the art of deception, and an entertainer.

Morton Smith in *Jesus the Magician: Charlatan or Son of God?* presents the case for viewing Jesus with suspicion. Smith points out that Jesus was a magician in the same way as another wandering sage of the times. This other sage, Apollonius of Tyana, known as a "divine man," was a follower of Pythagoras and a healer. According to Smith, "Apollonius came too close to Jesus for comfort."[32] The third-century writings that compare and contrast Apollonius and Jesus indicate that early Christians considered Apollonius to be a direct competitor of Jesus. Apollonius' work is well documented and he lived a long life. His existence and work as revealed by Smith can still be seen as a threat to Jesus Christ's validity.

I don't see the existence of Appolonius as a threat or even as some kind of smear on Jesus. I see Apollonius' work as proof that Messianic power is something we all have. We all are potential Magicians. We all are potential Messiahs. Christians accept Jesus as "the" Messiah. Jesus is not the only Messiah to have ever existed. Apollonius appears to be someone else who achieved Messianic consciousness. According to the Messianic teachings, we are all potential Messiahs. Every human being who exhibits Messianic power should be celebrated as another example of our potential. Apollonius' existence confirms Christ's teachings.

Physicists today embrace the thinking that all human beings have the potential to wield the power to heal and to mentally transcend time and place. The placebo effect—such as the power of sugar pills to "cure" illness—shows us that belief is powerful medicine. Statistically, the placebo is more powerful than any other pill.

Some researchers are even beginning to wonder if any medicine is a real cure. In *The Holographic Universe,* Michael Talbot documents numerous cases of people who healed themselves and others.[33] Talbot also discusses irrefutable cases of people who "knew" things were going to happen before they happened. Time is an illusion that exists because we believe it does. Our minds can expand beyond our physical "box" of five senses, and scientific explanation for our "out there" power is taking form. Miracles are not impossible. Our belief has full power over our reality.

Belief that creates a reality is magic. Illusions designed to instigate belief are magic misused. False profit reports on a stock market issue are magic misused. Terrorist attacks and what are called "false flag" operations are magic misused.

It is well documented that Paul and his fellow apostles would challenge pagan gods in their temples to outdo the miracles of their one God. What is not documented is the exact nature of the feats their one God performed to impress the crowds. We know that they were effective and that the pagan statues never answered or outdid any of the apostles' miracles.[34] We don't know how many of the scripture's miracle stories are symbolic and how many are true workings of the Light. It really doesn't matter. Belief is all. Belief does cure physical illness. Belief does bring about miraculous happenings. The basis of the belief, the motive behind the magic that's used, is what matters. Any belief wields power over our material existence. The motive behind the belief dictates the honor or dishonor in what we create.

We wield magic every moment of our lives. Yet this concept is foreign to us. Manly P. Hall, founder of the Philosophical Research Society in Los Angeles, tackled this reality. The following is from his *Magic, A Treatise on Esoteric Ethics:*

> Magic is the art of manipulating the unseen forces of nature.
>
> The black magician's motto is: "might is right" (survival of the fittest).
>
> The white magician's motto is: "right is might" (survival of all).
>
> Grey magic is the unconscious or subconscious perversion of power.
>
> Yellow magic is the failure to learn how to prevent the perversion of power.
>
> Black magic is the use of spiritual powers to gratify animal or selfish proclivities.
>
> White magic is the right use of spiritual power, consciously and objectively.[35]

When you take a good look at Hall's definitions, you realize that most of us practice yellow to grey magic, if not outright black magic. We practice in ignorance. Ignorance is the greatest evil of all. Yellow magic is practiced in laziness. Not paying attention results in our magic being used for purposes we would not support.

The Absolutes dictate that all of us wield magic. If we are not conscious of how our power is being used, someone else is directing it. If we fail to control our reflections of the Light, someone else will control them for us. Isolation stops others from using our power, but isolation perverts our power. A full, healthy life lived in honor of the Absolutes requires us to be conscious of our own power, lend it to work with others, and to raise ourselves and everyone else up to the highest consciousness, Messianic consciousness. To do this, you have to get involved. You have to take action in life. You have to work to influence your world.

The key to the Tree of Life is motivation, and this is true in Magic as well. Capitalism, working for personal profit, is black magic. I can hear the howls of outrage at this statement. Black magic is considered evil. Capitalism has brought the masses a lot of good. Of course it has; evil and good are different frequencies of the Light. The operation of the Light is all about balance. Capitalism can be white magic. An enterprise motivated by material gain alone is an enterprise based on black magic. All it takes is a shift in frequency, a change of motivation, to turn it around. The enterprise has to be based on more than personal or monetary gain. The enterprise must be for the good of mankind.

Black magic is using the power of the Light for personal gain. To do this requires refracting and blocking the Light to harness it to your will. Manipulating the good of all for the good of self counters the dictates of the Absolutes. Countering the Absolutes means killing rather than creating. Killing the Light is not possible. You can kill people who reflect the Light in ways you do not like. You can block the Light. You can refract the Light. You can shift and dodge the Light, but the Light always reconfigures to work for the good of all. To triumph, black magicians adhere to "might makes right." Black magicians have to kill people who refuse to reflect and block the Light in the way they want.

Jesus Christ stood for "right makes might." Jesus Christ was crucified. Jesus Christ stood in the way of the black magicians, the Money Power, of his time.

Money creation is a Magic power. In the teachings about the workings of Magic, the power of creation in material form is split into four fields: fire, air, water, and earth. As the study of Magic has evolved, the four fields have been symbolized respectively as swords, wands, cups, and pentagrams. Swords symbolize the field of might. Wands symbolize the field of creation. Cups symbolize the field of benevolence. Pentagrams symbolize the field of material wealth.

Money is a vital tool in all four fields. First, money wields the power of the sword. As Deuteronomy 23:21 teaches, lending money to landowners will result in the land eventually going to the lender. Second, money wields the power of the wand; money is valuable because we say it is. Third, money is a tool for benevolence. Gifting money is a primary act of benevolence. And fourth, money is material wealth. Money is a Magician's primary tool. Money is a magic wand.

The sources used for teaching esoteric Magic are the same sources Christ used to develop his teachings.[36] Practicing Magic is practicing adherence to the Absolutes of the Light. Adherence brings mankind the ability to mentally manifest physical change. We have the power; we reflect the Light. We combine our reflections with like reflections to increase our power to manifest and change our existence. We reflect the power of creation and the conditions of our existence.

Adhering to the Absolutes of the Light is to work toward Messianic consciousness. The work of Jesus was based on righting that which is upside down in the teachings of the Light. Jesus taught that "right makes might." Jesus Christ was the greatest white magician who ever lived. Jesus was nonviolent except in one instance. In a fit of rage, Jesus is said to have "overturned the tables of the money changers and the seats of those who were selling doves."[37] Jesus wanted to change how money worked. The temple priests and scribes began plotting to have Jesus put to death after his outburst. The Money Power was responsible for the crucifixion of Jesus Christ.

The money changers were charging exorbitant fees to exchange coins stamped with the faces of Roman emperors for shekels that had no image of an "idol" on them. Shekels were the only coins accepted as offerings at the temple and the money changers had cornered the market on them, making great profits with their monopoly. The temple authorities received a cut of the profits in spite of the fact that usury is listed in Psalms 15:5 as one of the offenses that will keep people out of God's kingdom. In Judaic law, money is to be lent as assistance to the poor in their distress, not as an investment. The way money is used is a point of honor. Making money off the poor by charging interest is forbidden.

Biblically, there are no provisions for "exorbitant" versus allowable interest rates. Money earned from the creation, use, exchange, handling, or lending of money is usury and thus forbidden. The temple authorities were operating under a loophole in the law found in Deuteronomy 23:20-21. This passage condones making money from lending to non-Jewish people or from non-Jewish practi-tioners of usury. This is a teaching that makes money a sword to be used to conquer "others." It is a "might makes right" doctrine.

When Jesus took on the priests' interpretation of usury law, he was taking on the Messianic doctrine of "might makes right" which was widely accepted at the time. Jesus turned the Hebrew teachings of a Messiah who wields a sword to do the will of the Light upside down. Jesus adhered to "right makes might." "Right" to Jesus meant rejecting the delineation between the "chosen" people and all other people. From Jesus Christ's perspective, the Money Power's practice of usury in the temple was an abomination of the workings of the Light. Usury dishonors the Absolutes. Differentiating between people dishonors the Absolutes. Making it OK to make money off money with some people but not others furthers the dishonor.

Contrary to the expected Messiah who would return Jerusalem to the Hebrews via the sword, Jesus came as a Messiah who preached Love as the "sword" of the Light. He preached that all were his brothers and sisters in the Light.

There is evidence in the Bible that Jesus was surrounded and supported by "zealots," armed mercenaries who were involved in militant uprisings against Rome. Many biblical scholars have noted the "zealot" label attached to both Simon the Zealot and Judas. There is sound theory that Jesus was crucified because of his association with these zealots who were wanted by Rome for past insurrections.[38]

Jesus preached nonviolence and the good of all mankind as the ultimate realization of Messianic consciousness. Nonviolence was not and still isn't the accepted interpretation of many who adhere to Messianic teachings. Not all the "zealots" who followed Jesus accepted love as the ultimate "sword" to use in doing the work of the Light. To this day, not all who follow Jesus Christ have accepted the "right makes might" dictate.

Leaders who chose to rule by the sword dominate much of the last two thousand years of church history. Political leaders who choose to rule by the sword are the norm to this day. Neither the separation of church and state nor Darwin's "survival of the fittest" theory of evolution is "evil" in intent or purpose, but their combined influence has enabled black magicians to operate openly and without impunity. Observe current economic, political and military actions around the world today; "might makes right" rules.

In the time of Jesus, the Money Power that held to the power of the sword as Messianic right was not of one ethnicity, of one religion, or of one nation any more than bankers and politicians are one kind in today's world. As obvious as this truth is, there has been a historical manipulation of who is at work behind the Money Power's operations. The Jewish people, because of their "loophole" in the practice of usury, have been both party to and victim of blame and manipulation through the centuries. The climax of the blame game happened in the World War II era.

For centuries, the Jewish people had no homeland. I believe this had to do with their way of dealing with Jewish law. By choice, historically, the Jewish people live separate from non-Jews. They do not/did not allow outsiders into their circle of intimacy. This practice protects/protected their law, which promotes the health and prosperity of all the Jewish people. Those who are not "God's chosen people," non-Jews, are/were treated with a different set of laws. In particular, the loophole in the usury law treated non-Jews differently from Jews. Usury was forbidden to the Roman Catholics as well as to the people of Islam, so this little loophole was useful to the host nations in which the Jewish people lived.[39]

Throughout the Middle Ages, kings who found themselves in financial difficulties would invite the Jewish people into their kingdoms to "fix" their economy. Once the nation was back in good economic condition, they would throw out the Jewish people, often violently.[40] Russia as well as England, Spain, Italy, and most other European nations engaged in this kind of relationship.

The self-imposed isolation of the Jewish people strikes me as very important. What started as a Jewish practice of self-protection evolved into imposed isolation and invited oppressive abuse from outsiders. By the 1500s, starting in Venice, Italy, the countries hosting Jewish communities began creating sections called "ghettos." Laws dictated the movements of the Jewish population into and out of these sections, enabling continued economic interaction while isolating Jews in their lifestyles and beliefs.[41]

Such isolation is counter to the tenth Absolute that we are all one. The Light works in an alternating pattern. If we resist the tenth Absolute and we choose to protect our own and keep "others" out, our own loses value and others will lash out against us. Treating others differently than you treat yourself and reaping violence in return is a reflection of the Light operating just as the Absolutes say it will. Usury is black magic. To continue the practice is going to require people killing each other at some time or other.

The laws of the Jewish community are laws that support the health and wealth of every member of the community. While the Absolutes dictate that joining together with each other on similar frequencies increases our power on those frequencies, the good of all is always the underlying dictate. To prosper in isolation with overt rejection of outsiders evokes resentment. In the case of the Hebrews, resentment festered and eventually turned into blame for the lack of prosperity in non-Jewish communities. Claiming to be "God's chosen people" and treating all "others" with a different code of conduct dishonors the Absolutes of the Light.

Claiming to be God's chosen people is hubris. The Jewish community set itself up to be the scapegoat for all the wrongs of the world by isolating itself. The establishment of a Jewish homeland, the state of Israel, simply repeats the "ghetto" of old. The difference is that now the ghetto has a military to enforce the isolation.

When I expressed this opinion to two concentration camp survivors who came to speak to my freshman class at Marymount College in New York in 1979, I caused serious shock and affront. I do not mean to cause distress. I do not mean to cause pain. It is time to be free of the old patterns that keep the pain and distress alive. All nations, communities, and religions must say and do for others as they say and do for themselves. I stand by my opinion on this matter.

I do not condone the operations of the Third Reich. Anti-Semitism is abhorrent, but so is the claim to being God's chosen people. The intolerance that led to the Holocaust was two-sided. We are all the sons and daughters of God. We are all descended from the same DNA. Germans suffered horrifying economic abuse. This abuse destroyed their economy not once but twice in the last century. The Jewish people were not responsible for the abuse. Dishonor of the Absolutes was responsible for the abuse. Authorities who believed they had superior right and greedy economic manipulators were responsible for the abuse. Inclusion, equal treatment for all mankind, is the true spiritual teaching and neither side in World War I or World War II Germany operated on that frequency.

Dishonor supported by ideas of superiority continues to this day. Dishonor supported by the "might makes right" dictate continues to this day. Nothing has changed. We are still engaging in war.

Adolf Hitler consciously used Messianic teachings. He was a "black magician," as are the bankers involved in funding wars. *The Messianic Legacy* tracks the Messianic teachings from their kabbalah beginnings through the royal houses of the Middle Ages and into modern-day politics. Hitler consciously manipulated Messianic teachings to build his Nazi party.[42] Mass psychology is the new name for Messianic use of power, the new name for Magic. "Mind games," magic, was used by Nazi party leaders to ensnare followers.

With Nazism, Adolf Hitler tapped into his people's need for transcendence; he created a new religion. No Messiah of this nature, a combined "high priest" and military force, had existed in the West since the emperors of Rome.

To tap into the hearts and minds of the German people the Nazi party meticulously orchestrated religion's most ancient techniques. As *The Messianic Legacy* describes, the Nazis used chanting, rhythmic repetition, charismatic oration, color, sexual energy, and light. In the ceremony that blessed new flags, a literal "insemination of the flags" was enacted. Hitler would take "die Blutfahne"—the party's most sacred relic, a Nazi flag stained with the blood of sixteen original members who died when they stood with Hitler in his first attempt to seize power—and vigorously thrust it at and over new flags, consecrating them with the blood-soaked original. "As if by a grotesque form of sexual magic," the book's authors tell us, "the sacred quality of the original flag was transferred to the new."[43]

Hitler's use of Messianic power was carefully managed. He elicited transcendental bliss in his audience. These techniques that use light and rhythm are effective. They are evident in Christian gatherings, revivals, political conventions, and rock concerts. Roman Catholic Masses sometimes manage to bring participants into states of altered consciousness. The communion ceremony was designed to raise each participant's consciousness to experience Absolute oneness.

The desire for Absolute oneness, the desire for spiritual ascendance, is programmed into our genes. We are all seekers, driven to reconnect to that which is greater than ourselves. We are all susceptible to being seduced and manipulated. As *The Messianic Legacy* authors say, Hitler tapped into his followers' genetic disposition for communal ascendance:

> What one witnessed at Hitler's rallies is an "alteration of consciousness" such as psychologists generally associate with a mystical experience. And Hitler himself becomes a black Messiah, acting as a receptacle for the religious energy he has evoked. In the words of one commentator, "It was not long before the German people began to see Hitler as a Messiah of Germany."
>
> ...The mayor of Hamburg is on record as saying, "We need no priests, we can communicate

> direct to God through Adolf Hitler" and in April, 1937, a conclave of German Christians declared, "Hitler's word is God's Law, the decrees and laws which represent it possess divine authority."[44]

Hitler studied Messianic teachings and Magic. Hitler used the Absolutes of the Tree of Life to create his vision of the "perfect" society. His ideal was a national socialist society. If we want to avoid being sucked into following a black messiah in the future, we need to recognize our own disposition to accept a "might makes right" dictate.

Black magic is a cancer in our spirituality. The potential for a healthy cell to mutate into a cancerous growth is constant. Our lifestyles, our exposure to toxins, and our genetic predispositions dictate the cell's potential to mutate. Our spiritual circumstances affect our choice between "might makes right" and "right makes might" in a similar way.

Healthy cells and cancerous cells in the body are different manifestations of the same thing, human cells. Good and evil are different manifestations of the same thing, human reflections of the Light. Good and evil as the same thing is reflected again in the Messianic workings of mass psychology.

Descriptions of Hitler's rallies in *The Messianic Legacy* mirror what it's like to go to a rock concert. John Lennon was not so off the mark when he said the Beatles were more popular than Jesus Christ.[45] It is not sacrilege to say this. Jesus Christ was trying to teach us all to be Messiahs. Jesus Christ tried to raise humanity to full Messianic consciousness. I honestly believe if Jesus had heard John Lennon's statement, he would have agreed that Lennon was right. He would also protest the Beatles' unfair advantage; Jesus didn't have electric music and public broadcasting to amp up the frequencies of his message.

Religion, politics, music, and everything that brings us together are Messianic forces. Motivation and purpose dictate the magic performed when we come together. Motivation and purpose are "frequencies." We are bodies electric and we operate on and are affected by frequencies.

My first development project out of film school was inspired by a working Tesla coil at the Griffith Observatory in Los Angeles. This coil broadcasts electricity. When turned on, it lights up a bulb six feet away. While watching a demonstration of the coil, my mind latched onto the physical influence broadcasted power in electric music might have on human frequencies. Jimi Hendrix's refrain, "Excuse me while I kiss the sky"[46] took on a whole new depth of meaning for me.

Your body moves because your mind sends electric signals from your brain to your body parts telling them to move. Brain-wave frequencies are identifiable. Broadcast electricity frequencies are equally identifiable. Broadcast electricity frequencies can be tuned to brain-wave frequencies. Broadcast electricity could be used for mind control.

Watching the Tesla coil filled my imagination with implied potentials for control of the masses. My mind leaped to the physical as well as spiritual connections that were being tapped with electric music. The potential for the authoritarian abuse of humanity is overwhelming.

In doing further research, I found that Nikola Tesla, creator of this coil, discovered and introduced us to the frequencies of power that surround us and power us. His work in the early twentieth century was mindblowing. He showed us that we are "bodies electric," that our bodies, our minds, and our actions all translate into frequencies. His patents include radio, remote control, and human frequency identifications. In essence, his work is responsible for most of the technology we use today. His landmark work was the demonstration and clarification of the fact that electricity travels in an alternating current pattern. His findings, when applied to life, go far beyond giving us a more efficient way to deliver electricity and communications.

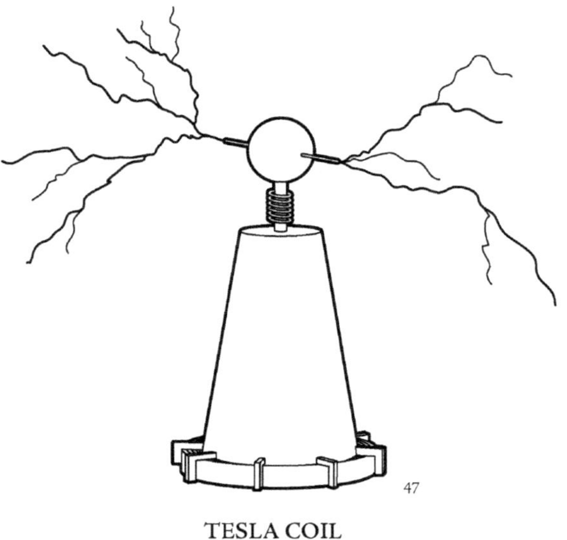

TESLA COIL

Alternating current reflects "What goes around comes around," or "Treat others as you would have them treat you," or the yin and yang of Chi. Tesla demonstrated that this spiritual base applies not only to all levels of power—electric, light, and sound—but literally to human frequencies. He demonstrated that all of life and material matter has a frequency, that even the earth itself has a frequency, and that all frequencies are interconnected.[48] All of existence is connected by this natural principle of reciprocity.

Spiritual teachings suddenly become rational physical science when seen in the light of Tesla's findings. My linking of Jimi Hendrix's "kiss the sky" lyric with broadcast electricity's hypothetical ability to be used for mind control mirrors the teachings of the ancient mystery schools.

Around 500 B.C., the philosopher Pythagoras discovered the harmonics of music and the numerical patterns of harmonics. He taught that our human patterns of speech and action are connected with the harmonics of nature. According to Pythagoras, all can be correlated to a number. Sir Isaac Newton devised his view of the workings of the universe from Pythagoras's numerical view.[49]

Modern science in general ridicules the Pythagorean idea of applying numerical values to aspects of life. This practice has evolved into numerology. Numerology, we can all readily agree, is not a science. But with frequency identifications, Pythagoras was not that off base. The frequencies we emit with our speech and actions do have a measurable impact on the world. Frequencies have exact numerical correlations.

Quantum physicists are only beginning to understand the full power of our personal frequencies. With every new finding, the differences between the spiritual mysteries' Absolutes and scientific facts are disappearing. Physicists have discovered quarks, tiny particles of matter that do things because we expect them to. They appear because we are looking for them.[50] This is the ninth Absolute; all that we want will manifest. Paying attention is key.

The power that frequencies and energy waves have over us is unquestionably immense. This power makes it imperative that the law of the land be that the people own the airwaves. The airwaves must be maintained for the good of all. Laws put in place to do this have slowly been whittled away. Subliminal advertising, for example, was heavily discussed and warned against in my youth. The power of planted suggestions in broadcast content was seen as a potential evil. Today, every television show and movie has "product placement." We the People are not paying attention. Our homes are being infiltrated with "you're not good enough until you have this" messages. We the People do not question the frequencies with which we are being bombarded.

In the 1980s, studies conducted by Bryce Gyngell, former chairman of Australia's Broadcasting Tribunal, showed that watching television shuts down the right side of the brain, the questioning side. Every broadcast frequency influences our brain-wave frequencies. Television broadcasts literally alter our brain waves in such a way that we do not question information.[51]

Gyngell's studies concluded that people who fall asleep while watching TV have a better innate ability to protect themselves from unquestioned input. Most of us stay awake while viewing, completely oblivious to the fact that we are being "brainwashed."

Most of us live with our frequencies in the "mud." Mud is the term used by broadcast engineers to describe a signal with light levels or frequencies too low to produce a clear, clean picture. Thus, we do not know our own power. Only awake and aware individuals have the power to lessen the amount of energy an outside force can channel from their minds. Only people who have worked to pay attention, to raise their own frequencies out of the "mud," can resist entering into a negative, unproductive existence that leaves them prone to having their energies used by others for purposes they don't support.

Full interface with the Light clarifies our frequencies. Realizing our individual interface with the Light requires regular disengagement from social and political reflections. Meditation, for example, clarifies perceptions. Regular introspection and disengagement from social and political forces are essential to staying out of the mud and maintaining individual liberty. Freedom requires freethinkers. Mud thinkers destroy the land of the free by rote. Unquestioning routine and suppression of individualized action stagnates freedom and our ascendance to the kingdom of God.

Mud thinking is conditioned. Oppression, judgments, and stereotypes clog our frequencies. The mud percolates under the surface of our psyches as individuals and in society as a whole. The statement that "Jews are responsible for all of wars in the world" is a good example of mud thinking. The blame statement has been used for centuries to cover up what has really been responsible for all the wars of the world: the Money Power. The Jews are not the Money Power. They have been key practitioners of Money Power theory, but they have not been alone as the authorities, leaders, or kings who have wielded the Money Power in the world.

Today's "kings"—that is, today's Money Power and mass psychology shapers—wield the entertainment industry and the military industrial complex.

Economist and lecturer Dr. Stuart Crane tells us, "The purpose of war is to create debt and to extract wealth from the slobs who don't know how to use it into the hands of those that do [the Elite]."[52] We have to become conscious of the Magicians at work in our lives and behind the wars on earth. Histories of the end of WWI mention the wheelbarrows of money needed just to buy a loaf of bread in Germany. Money is the Magician's tool. If we allow superior "kings" to dictate how our money is to be valued, we are at the mercy of their honor.

When the honor of a Money Power proves corrupt, unworthy of trust or is destroyed, the belief in the money's value disappears.

Resorting to usury or raising interest rates can stanch distrust in a currency's value. Raising interest rates can save the integrity of a currency in the eyes of world Money Powers. Raising interest rates causes people to lose their homes, businesses, and jobs. Recession and depression are direct results of corrupt Money Powers manipulating monetary policy to save themselves from ruin. The population the money was created to serve suffers ruin in the interest of preserving the Money Power.[53] The current Chairman of the United States Federal Reserve, Ben Bernanke, calls this aspect of the workings of money "the moral hazard."

The alternative to raising interest rates is to print more money. Inflation is a sign that corruption has taken root in a money supply.

Corruption is the visible sign of the cancer called "might makes right" before it kills. The extent of the corruption determines how long it takes for a currency to become worthless. The extent of a cancer's growth determines how long a person will live. When monetary authorities refuse to cease corrupt practices or they become trapped and over-burdened by inflation and interest rates, war breaks out.

If you want to know why a war is being waged, pay attention to how money is being created and used to control mankind. Knowing the world's monetary workings is how we divine the truth of conflict and observe humanity's workings with the Light.

Money is our magic wand. Money reflects our material power. Who we give our power to, who gives power to us, and the work we do directly impacts our progress on the paths that lead to Messianic consciousness. The way money works reflects the kind of kingdom we are. The way money works reflects mankind's state of consciousness. The way money works is within We the People's control.

Taking responsibility for power is dependent upon taking responsibility for our consciousness. The three base Absolutes are:

- we all have equal power to reflect the Light;
- we are autonomous in the use of this power; and
- if we combine forces with like-minded reflectors of the Light,
  we raise our power accordingly.

We have to pay attention to our own power. We have to pay attention to whom we are lending our power. We have to question authority and those to whom we lend our power. We choose between leading our lives via "right makes right" or "might makes right" dictate according to whom and what we lend our power.

Ghettos, churches, and political parties exist because people lend them their power. What starts out as a "right" enterprise can easily turn into a "might makes right" enterprise. The desire to have power over others and the desire to hang onto control can change our motivations in an instant. Motive is the key to Magic. As Hall says, "Even the greatest of white magicians can become a degenerate or black magician in an instant if his motive becomes unworthy. The white magician serves humanity; the black magician seeks to serve himself."[54]

Our families are our first line of power interface. Our choice of "might makes right" versus "right makes might" is first made at home. Our parents and our families condition our mode of operation. Unfortunately, healthy family conditioning is rare. Which dictate, "might" or "right," should take priority is not clear-cut for most of us. Our autonomy, our physical health, and our ability to transcend to higher consciousness all depend on rational consciousness. Rational consciousness depends on our family's psychological health.

I've found studying psychological health and family therapy to be incredibly enlightening. Mental health, freedom from oppression, and unconditional love play important roles in our ability to achieve personal power. Money is our magic wand, but money is useless if we perceive ourselves as powerless. Public figures with great wealth prove this all the time. The tabloids thrive by reflecting the powerlessness of those who have money.

For the last eight years, I've been a coordinator of continuing education courses for psychologists. My responsibilities include attending and monitoring these courses. When I videotape them, I almost memorize these courses in the editing process. The one overriding conviction I have formed is that the basis for mental health is personal power. There is no mental illness without the perception of personal powerlessness. The degree of self-perceived powerlessness directly contributes to the severity of a person's mental illness. Family, intimates, and personal associates are key to maintaining one's sense of power.

Family and family lines have always been essential to Messianic thinking. Kings typically inherit from their father's line, and alternative families with equal traditional Messianic power have always existed. When a family line failed to produce heirs, there were other families with equal power to turn to. Bloodlines became revered and descendents from "Grail kings" ruled by right of birth. I believe the whole blood thing is mud thinking. Consciousness makes a Messiah. Family consciousness is "knowing" at work in the family tree, and it mirrors the Light at work in the Tree of Life.

Family power is Messianic power at work in our lives. Our family relationships directly impact our personal power and our perception of power. Unconditional acceptance, love as dictated by the seventh Absolute, is crucial to our being able to achieve wholeness and be effective magicians, Messiahs. Our family's wholeness directly impacts our personal wholeness.

CHAPTER 4
Personal Power Starts In The Family

It's a Family Affair

In 1972, Sly and the Family Stone sang about blood being thicker than mud in "It's a Family Affair."[55] Blood—family—can be worse than mud for our personal frequencies.

Mud, for video broadcast engineers, is a signal that's not strong enough to produce a clear picture. When light frequencies are weak, we get a "muddy" picture. When our family's intimate connections are scattered and inattentive, we are living in mud. Family connections should be and can be the clarifier of the mud, but first we have to attain unconditional acceptance of each member of our family.

Just as the Creator God has been used to subjugate mankind, parental dictate has been used to subjugate us as individuals. But if we pay attention to family and honor unconditionally who our family members are and who we are, God can become love and family can free us.

The ties that bind family have been used to manipulate and dominate both parents and their children for centuries. Society fully accepts that parents' needs and wants must be put aside for the good of their children. In turn, children are conditioned to honor their parents' wishes and follow their parents' will before their own. Adherence to family expectations and to accepted workings of society often creates an overwhelming sense of powerlessness. Family can block our ascendance to Messianic consciousness.

In the Bible, we find that Jesus was unable to perform miracles in his hometown. The people who knew Jesus best refused to believe he could perform miracles. Thus, he couldn't. Faced with this power block, in the Gospel of Mark, Jesus declares, "A prophet is not without honor except in his native place among his own kin and his own house."[56]

This interplay of personal power and family is why Jesus Christ said, "If anyone comes to me and does not hate his own father and mother and wife and children and brothers and sisters, yes, and even his own life, he cannot be my disciple."[57] The intimate interactions between family members are our strongest attachments to material existence. They are the most common blocks to our ascendance. Family members oppress us because we believe they're supposed to. They're not.

Belief is everything in our existence. What we believe is what will be. Belief manifests reality. Belief can ensure the full realization of our power, or belief can block us from full realization of our power. What people believe about us affects what we believe about ourselves. What we believe about ourselves is what we become. Family can be and should be the source of our empowerment. Family should be the base that supports our freedom. Family members are supposed to believe in each other. Family members are supposed to believe in themselves.

As with everything in life, Magic and the Light and the truth require balance. Our personal power is dependent on how much power we are allowed to wield for ourselves in our family relationships. In this aspect, the family tree mirrors the Tree of Life.

In the kabbalah course I took at the Philosophical Research Society, I learned that tarot cards are reflections of the paths of the Tree of Life. There's a tradition of laying out the tarot cards along specific paths of the Tree.[58] In the highest reaches of the Tree of Life, in the forces of the "Trinity," you find that the Fool card and the Magician card are equals. The Fool is symbolic of the path that emanates out of what is called the Ain Soph Aur, the limitless Light that is the source of All. The Magician is symbolic of the path that is the full reflection of the Light back to the source.

Studying the juxtaposition of these paths led to my realization that the Magician and the Fool are equal. This discovery was a huge revelation for me. That we are all Fools is a given, but it was an eye-opener to find that, because the Fool is equal to the Master, we are all Magicians also, consciously or not.

The Light will manifest the needs of both the Magician and the Fool equally. By simply living according to the dictates of the Light, the Fool's material needs appear when needed. He unconsciously works magic and material result. Similarly, the Magician or Master—the person who understands the workings of the Light and models his or her work accordingly—will be conscious of the material result he or she has wrought.

Both the Magician and the Fool make miracles happen, one consciously, the other unconsciously. The power is always at work. The Messiah is the Magician, a person who has studied the working of the Light and can manipulate it with knowledge of the outcome. The Magician can be an unwitting Fool, just as the Fool can be an unwitting Magician, The outcome is the Light's prerogative. The Light is out of human control. The Light is the real Magician or Messiah. We can only reflect the Light.

The equality of the Fool and the Magician in realizing Messianic power is most evident when it comes to parenting. The Fool and the Magician make up the left hand and right hand of the "Holy Trinity" of paths. They also top what are often referred to as columns.

The power of the Light is balanced between these two columns. On the right, below the path of the Magician, is the column of severity; on the left, below the path of the Fool, is the column of mercy. Effective parenting requires the balance of the two. Too much discipline is as unhealthy as no discipline. Both extremes result in feelings of powerlessness and being unloved.

The good news for parents is that the balance of power of the Fool and the Magician manifests in what psychologists call the "good enough parent." Why do some kids with horrible home lives become successful and well balanced, while other kids with seemingly good home lives become unbalanced and without personal purpose? The answer is that the child who turns out well balanced had some adult in his or her childhood who was unconditionally accepting. The overall environment is less important. The "good enough parent" is the adult who never wavers in belief in and unconditional acceptance of the child. This "parent" could be a drug addict or a total mess-up in many other ways, but he or she remains "a good enough parent" by helping to minimize the refractions in the child's self-perception and self-esteem. What children need more than anything else is the freedom to reflect the Light the way they are born "knowing" how to do.

To live in full reflection of the Light is to live in a constant state of being loved. To be loved is to be fully accepted, empowered. The Light is the only constant source of love and power. Families by their nature are not perfect; refractions are inevitable. We are all familiar with the whole range of negative experiences in our families. Jealousy, distrust, resentment, anger, disappointment, and dishonor are results of feeling unloved and powerless. The pain resulting from these less than loving refractions multiplies. Such pain sets the pattern for oppression and abuse that dictates the dynamic of a family's functioning. Patterns of oppression and abuse carry on into each member's relationships with the rest of the world.

Let's take a family that prides itself on sharp wit. Every show of ignorance or slow perception at home is met with derision and taunting. A child in this family who tends to daydream and create alternative mental connections can be a constant object of negative attention and teasing. A child subjected to this kind of treatment will tend to develop a negative self-image and/or suffer from depression. This child will echo the pattern and develop a habit of belittling and criticizing himself or herself and others. If this child never meets anyone who validates his or her talents and strengths, the abuse of others escalates, and symptoms of mental imbalance begin to present.

Patterns of oppression and abuse exist in the most loving families. Cultural patterns, prejudiced patterns, sexual patterns, sexist patterns, and other learned behaviors that cross generations are tolerated and on the surface don't cause problems. That these patterns are oppression is not commonly recognized. Oppression is not a word most of us readily identify with. It's something that happens to "others." We don't recognize that we oppress ourselves with our own views and patterns of behavior. I never considered myself "oppressed." A few inappropriate sexual innuendos in my career don't count as oppression.

Most people feel that they are free from oppression, most white people anyway. People of color can tell you all about external oppression, but they too do not readily identify self-oppression or what is known as internalized oppression.

Our understanding of oppression is that it happens from forces outside of us; it comes from the prejudices, ignorance, and fear of people different from ourselves. We believe the oppressed are not to blame. People don't oppress themselves. I've learned differently. Oppression happens if the oppressed accept the oppression. The oppressed have to internalize the "rightness" of the oppression for it to exist. When women believe they are dependent, when people of color believe they are given less opportunity, when blondes believe they are dumber, when boys believe they are stronger, they bring the belief to form in reality. Our own perception of personal limitation holds our Absolute power in captivity.

My enlightenment regarding self-oppression occurred while I participated in United to End Racism (UER) workshops in 2005 in Los Angeles. My Re-evaluation Counseling group, a private organization that operates in tandem with UER, held meetings titled "Whites Eradicating Racism" once a month over the year.[59] I learned that racism is just one of the forms of oppression that we manifest every day of our lives. Oppression starts the moment we identify "others."

It startled me to realize that thinking my sister or a teacher was better than me somehow was oppression. I had never thought of my automatic judging of someone looking good or being smarter as a form of oppression. Thinking of anyone who is "other" than us as better or worse is oppression. The eradication of oppression depends on us accepting that we are all good. All is good.

The attendees were multicultural and all races were accounted for, yet the meeting title was "Whites Eradicating Racism." Is this not a racist title? Are whites responsible for causing or ending racism? Is it white people's fault that racism exists? We all have internalized differentiation between humans, and we accept unspoken valuations of these differentiations.

Self-oppression occurs when we judge ourselves superior to others just as much as it does when we judge ourselves inferior. Internalized racism—internalized value placed on types of people—is not a comfortable reality to have to face. There is an unspoken rank assigned to the different forms of the human race, first whites, then Asians and Latinos. Blacks usually end at the bottom. Asians, blacks, and Latinos would rank themselves differently. Then you have women. Men have more power than women. Asian men have intellectual power. Asians are often ranked superior to whites in intelligence. Latino men have cajones. Black men and white women are gaining equality. White women definitely have more power than women of color. We have to own our part in validating these kinds of differentiations. We have to recognize how we perceive ourselves within these valuations before we can eradicate them.

Our first exercise at the racism seminar was to recount our very first experience with the "other." This "other" is not always someone of a different race. For me, my first awareness of an undesirable "other" was in my immediate family. My mother is of Irish/German descent and my father is first-generation Italian American. They met and married in California. By not marrying an Italian, Dad married outside his family's ideal. For my father's family, my mother was the "other." My paternal grandfather, Salvatore, never forgave her for calling my brother Joe instead of naming my brother for him. She did this because she didn't want my brother to be an "other" to his peers. Salvatore was not a name she was comfortable with. My mother was always an outsider among the women in my father's family. At the same time, my father was an "other" to my mother's family. My maternal grandmother called him and his family "Eyetalians."

The unspoken valuation of these family differences became terror for me when I was five years old and we were visiting my father's aunt's family in Brooklyn. I was to sleep with my cousin Anne Marie in her room. Anne Marie and I were close, but sleeping in her room was too close for comfort. To me, she was one of the "others" who caused so much discomfort in my mother's life. I became hysterical, and nothing would induce me to sleep near her. I had internalized identification with my mother's family. My Irish/German ancestry was "better." I was experiencing the irrational fear of becoming an "other," an "Eyetalian" by association.

Irrational, hysterical terror of being an "other" overcame me again a year or two later when my family was living in South America. My father was working for IBM, which was developing a manufacturing plant in Montevideo, Uruguay. We took an extended trip up the Amazon River. Naked children swam along the boat, begging and diving for coins. These children shocked me. The extreme poverty of the people we encountered was overwhelming.

My mother explained that the American monetary system was why US citizens didn't live in these kinds of extreme conditions. I took comfort in my "superiority" and the understanding that the extreme discrepancy in life circumstances I was witnessing was not my fault; "they" lived in an inferior social system.

After a morning shooting iguanas from our dugout canoes, we arrived in a little village with houses on stilts. We took turns posing with our fresh kills before giving them to the residents to eat. There was a girl my age in the village with a tortoise in her arms. As everyone took pictures, I was asked to pose with her. The thought that I was being equated to this "other" girl drove me to hysterics. I refused to cooperate.

This terror of being an "other" finally lifted from me when I was about nine years old. I was in an outdoor farmers market in Uruguay around Christmas time. A vendor struck up a conversation, starting with the confirmation that I was from the United States. I'd lived in Uruguay for three years by this time and was somewhat fluent in Spanish. We discussed the differences in the countries, especially in the ways we celebrated the holidays. Uruguayans set off fireworks at Christmas. I can remember feeling time suspend. I could see the Light in this man's eyes. He was just like me. The Light was the same. All people have this same Light inside. The terror of being identified as an "other" never returned.

The root of the oppression in our family wasn't clear to me until years later when my father's mother died in the early 1980s. My father returned with an old photograph after helping his sisters clear out their mother's house. I took a look at the picture. It was of a dark-skinned, dark-eyed family, circa the end of the nineteenth century. I asked my father who the people were. He said it was the Puerto Rican family who had lived next door to them in Brooklyn. I accepted this and passed the picture to my sister, who was much less accepting. She looked at the picture and wanted to know why he had a picture of the Puerto Rican family from next door. At that Dad laughed and admitted it was his mother's family, newly arrived in America.

During the workshop as I recounted the tale of my father sharing the picture of his "Puerto Rican" family with me, I came to fully understand internalized racism. My father did not want to be an "other." He grew up in New York City not speaking English until he went to school. Puerto Ricans were the most despised "other" in Brooklyn when he grew up. He probably had to disown being one many times. He worked hard to lose his Brooklyn accent when he moved to California; he was not like "them," those despised Puerto Ricans. He married a fair-skinned American girl who had no "old country" ties. I internalized my father's fear and did not want to be like "them," the ethnic people. The "all-American" white girl was my preferential identification. I was a California girl.

All of us have internalized this fear of being classified as an undesirable "other." Neighborhoods have unspoken norms. We don't want to live next door to an "other." To live next door to an "other" would mean that it could then be inferred that we are an "other." What we do not realize is that this conditioning is oppressing us. Accepting that certain looks, colors, or shapes of people are superior to "others" oppresses our consciousness. Society as a whole accepts oppression. Skinny is better than fat. Tall is better than short. Clear skin is better than blemished skin. The list is long.

Loving parents oppress themselves. Parents repress their needs for the good of their children. Most of us accept this necessary oppression without question. We shouldn't. Oppression is not healthy. Oppression breeds anger and frustration. Parental oppression can be seen in parents who come down too hard on their children. The children get the brunt of their parents' frustration over not being able to pursue self-transcendence. Parents will do too much for their child and then, driven by fear that the child will not make anything of himself or herself, throw the child out of the house.

Parental frustration creates a cycle of oppression. The children become "burdens." Parents abort their own self-actualizations and they demand that their children do the same. Parental oppression makes it very difficult for families to love unconditionally.

Society supports this cycle of parental oppression because the "cross" parents bear is seen as a God-given burden. All the responsibility and pressure to make sure children turn out right is placed on the parents. "Good parents" can handle the job. Only unacceptable "others" fail to raise successful children on their own. This societal expectation dishonors the Messianic ideal.

A Messiah is one who is a shining example of how we can fully reflect the Light to create the reality we desire. If we accept that parenting means we must focus all of our power on our children, then we block our full potential to be Messiahs. In turn, we teach our children to block their full potentials.

A lot of attention has been given to mother oppression, but parental oppression hits men too. Even in homes with a traditional, full-time mother, fathers suffer from self-oppression. From the moment a couple says "I do," conditioned oppressions take root. Men will give up themselves for family, just as women will. The oppression is resented and anger is constant. The "furies" hound the parents, and the children get beaten down and verbally abused. Oppression is a vicious cycle that mires us in the "mud." If all of humanity is ever going to achieve Messianic consciousness, our acceptance of parental oppression has to be broken.

Understanding the power of being a "good enough parent" is the first step to breaking the cycle of parental and self-oppression. When you embrace imperfection as a parent, you make room for joy. With joy you can love unconditionally, knowing that your child is good. Parent oppression dies when you understand that you are a better parent when you work for your own transcendence first. Children do better when parents are "good enough." Parents do better when they do what they need to do for themselves, for their pursuit of happiness.

This understanding was a long time coming for me. My oldest child, Max, suffered the worst of my "supermom" attention. Doing too much for a child in the effort to be a perfect mom is not unusual. I just could not let go. I didn't get that my anger in the face of my son not doing what I expected him to do had more to do with me, my frustrations, and my lack of fulfilling my needs than anything he was doing or not doing. Letting go, taking care of your own work, and unconditionally believing in your children to take care of theirs is the true dictate of the Light. A good enough parent is one who has found the third pillar on the Tree of Life, the pillar of perfect balance.

On the paths of the Tree of Life, honor is reflected when the Light is fully balanced as it ascends back to the source. Honor in the family is reflected in a fully balanced family tree. A fully balanced family tree is one in which everyone works on attaining full consciousness, full autonomy, and full responsibility for mastering the Absolutes in their own lives. Individuals thrive and succeed when loved ones support them unconditionally. Individuals thrive and succeed when loved ones model thriving and succeeding.

CHAPTER 5

Personal Power And The Village

Pink Houses

Just as your family has the power to enable or disable your connection to the Light and your ascendance to Messianic consciousness, so too does your "village" enable or disable you and your family's freedom and power to actualize connection to the Light and Messianic consciousness.

The United States of America is the home of the free. It is a nation, a village, designed to enable you to pursue Messianic consciousness. In 1983, John Mellencamp celebrated that America is the home of the free in song; he added little pink houses for us all in his observation.[60] Little pink houses are the perfect symbol for the power our village has over our freedom.

Our need to connect with people of like minds to realize higher consciousness starts in the family and extends into society. What our neighbors, community, schools, and media do and think play parts in our freedom or lack of freedom of consciousness. Not all of us want to live in "little pink houses," but we will and do if it is what everyone else does. The village oppresses us as much as our families do.

I picked up Betty Friedan's *The Feminine Mystique* around the year 2000.[61] Much to my surprise, I discovered the most important element of oppression addressed by Friedan was how our society was being programmed to replace spiritual transcendence with material wealth. Friedan singled out the Money Power's influence on society's perception of self as key in the oppression of women.

Friedan documented advertising executives and think tank professionals who deliberately designed marketing campaigns to appeal to women's disposition to seek spiritual transcendence. Friedan revealed advertising campaigns designed to substitute spiritual growth with material satisfaction. This revelation of mass psychology being used to manipulate oppression surprised me. My experience with the women's rights movement had never included the concept that the media were colluding to replace our desire for spiritual transcendence with a desire to acquire material goods.

The feminist movement exploded when *The Feminine Mystique* was published in 1964. The public's focus quickly zoomed in on a woman's right to work. Women's need to be more, do more, have their own careers, and have equal opportunity to support themselves became a high-profile, worthy cause. A lot of good change has come from the women's rights movement, but change in marketing practices has not come about. Television is still a "you are not good enough until you have this product" voice in our homes. Attaining happiness via material wealth is the primary creative force at work in our "village," the United States today.

I assumed that Friedan's book ignited the movement for women's right to work. But that is not what Friedan's book is about. Friedan's book is about our need for spiritual transcendence, our need for freedom and how it is being undermined by mass psychology.

Friedan was calling our attention to the unhealthy affects of our nation's post WWII economic policy of consumption. The U.S. government and corporations combined to form a national policy of consumption designed to ramp up the U.S. economy. Retail analyst Victor Labow put the psychological operation involved in instilling consumption into words:

> Our enormously productive economy ... demands that we make

> consumption our way of life, that we convert the buying and use of goods into rituals, that we seek our spiritual satisfaction, our ego satisfaction, in consumption...we need things consumed, burned up, replaced and discarded at an ever-accelerating rate.[62]

Women, as Friedan revealed, were the advertising executives' prime target in this psychological paradigm. Women had the most time to shop.

The media focus on Friedan's message shifted attention to women's rights. I assumed that public sentiment and real need had simply progressed in a natural direction. The spiritual problem Friedan addressed remained the same. The practice of replacing our spiritual desire for freedom and transcendence with a compulsion to purchase goods dominates our society to this day. In fact, going to work outside the home simply increased women's purchasing power.

In 2006, an insidious perspective on what happened to Friedan's original cry for freedom came to my attention. I viewed an online interview with Aaron Russo. Russo, who died in 2007, was a film producer best known for his films *The Rose* and *Trading Places* and his 2006 documentary, *America, From Freedom to Fascism.* His work had come to focus almost exclusively on the Money Power in the United States.

Russo offered an alternative perspective of the women's lib era. This perspective was given to him in a conversation with a member of one of the most influential monetary families in the United States, Nick Rockefeller. Rockefeller is a member of the Council on Foreign Relations, the International Institute of Strategic Studies, the Advisory Board of RAND, the Pacific Council on International Policy, the Committee on Foreign Relations in Los Angeles, and the Western Justice Center, and served as a participant in the World Economic Forum and the Aspen Institute.

Russo says Rockefeller told him the Rockefeller Foundation was the force behind the media hype and newspaper stories that drove the women's lib movement. They funded the movement for two primary reasons:

> One reason was you couldn't tax half the population before women's lib and the second reason was, now you get the kids in school at an early age. You can indoctrinate the kids to think. This breaks up the family. The

> kids start looking at the state as their family.[63]

Whether Rockefeller really said this or not can be easily challenged. Russo's revelation is hearsay. That government and corporate interests use mass psychology to manipulate and sidetrack public issues is fact. This is how Messianic power works. It is also fact that powerful families raising whole human beings operating with full intelligence and honor is rare in the United States today. That our media have had a role in our families' frames of mind cannot be disputed either.

Our public media and news agencies have been in bed with the Money Power via the Central Intelligence Agency for decades. The CIA is not readily seen as a bankers' operation, but it is. The CIA is a Wall Street creation established to further the workings of the debt-based Money Power. This fact is startling to many US citizens.

Allen Dulles, the first civilian director of the CIA, was a Wall Street-backed operative working illegally to further the aims of investment bankers at the end of WWII. Congress made CIA activities legal and named the operation the Central Intelligence Agency two years after the Wall Street organizers had actually started operations.[64] The direct support US media companies give CIA operatives is a fact that was confirmed by noted author Carl Bernstein in an article for *Rolling Stone*:

> Among the executives who lent their cooperation to the Agency (the CIA) were William Paley of the Columbia Broadcasting System, Henry Luce of Time Inc., Arthur Hays Sulzberger of the *New York Times*, Barry Bingham Sr. of the *Louisville Courier-Journal* and James Copley of the Copley News Service. Other organizations which cooperated with the CIA include the American Broadcasting Company, the National Broadcasting Company, the Associated Press, United Press International, Reuters, Hearst Newspapers, Scripps-Howard, Newsweek magazine, the Mutual Broadcasting System, *The Miami Herald*, and the old *Saturday Evening Post* and *New York Herald-Tribune*. By far the most valuable of these associations, according to CIA officials, have been with *The New York Times*, CBS, and Time Inc.[65]

Our national media's mode of operation has not changed since 1977 when these revelations were published. If anything, the number of corporate controlling interests who dictate information policy has become even smaller.

We have to pay attention to what resonates as true reflections of the Light and what's a refraction of the Light in our lives. Our public media is a Money Power "spin" zone. We need to pay attention to who is talking and educate ourselves regarding their ideology and agenda.

The actual names of CIA operatives at work in the media are not readily available today. The names of members of consortiums like the Council of Foreign Relations, the Trilateral Commission, and the Bilderberg group were compiled in 1995.[66] These organizations' members include international government leaders, corporate CEOs, media owners, news professionals, educators, and writers who believe in unifying the world. They have a "one world" vision. David Rockefeller has played a leading role in directing all three of these organizations, as he says, "Some even believe we (the Rockefeller family) are part of a secret cabal working against the best interests of the United States, characterizing my family and me as 'internationalists' and of conspiring with others around the world to build a more integrated global political and economic structure—one world, if you will. If that's the charge, I stand guilty, and I am proud of it."[67] Rockefeller adheres to the "might makes right" mode of operation. Individuals achieving Messianic consciousness are not part of his agenda, unless the individuals work for him.

Zealotry is alive and well in the world. What is actually right is not always easily discerned. Messages that call on us to judge others are refractions designed to distract us from accurate discernment. "Might makes right" refractions are designed to add noise in our reception of the Light. Honor demands recognition that all is good. The Absolutes demand that we treat everyone and every thing as we would have them treat us. Without refraction, the Light's frequencies do not include judgment of others.

The social climate that evolved in response to the women's liberation movement was intensely judgmental. Women began to feel socially stigmatized if they didn't find careers outside the home. Higher consciousness needs were not addressed. Mass marketing zeal focused on women entering the workplace.

Media attention at the dawn of the women's liberation movement created a "battle of the sexes." Public tensions escalated; women burned their bras, and men were blamed for women's oppression. Spiritual questions were derided as another form of insidious oppression of women. Religious oppression was and still is blamed for forcing women into subservient roles in the home. As a teenager during this time, I saw the whole cause as righteous and just. What I overlooked and what I believe is still being overlooked is that desire for spiritual transcendence and religious oppression are two very different things. Spiritual transcendence requires change, harmonious change that raises our consciousness.

The national media's message did manipulate Friedan's message. Demanding that women gain the right to control their own money doesn't answer the original need voiced by Friedan. Increased purchasing power does not help women achieve spiritual transcendence. To this day our media manipulate us into thinking it does. Making money and spending money is how transcendence works in our nation. Material transcendence has replaced spiritual transcendence in our social psyche.

Livelihood does play a part in our transcendence. The work we do is key to the fourth Absolute. Right livelihood is essential to mastering transcendence. Right livelihood does not require making money. With right livelihood money comes because that is how the Absolutes work. The women's liberation movement is an example of good and evil being the same thing on different frequencies. Much good has come for women. Our choices for livelihood are much greater, and our right to pursue our autonomy free of harassment is better enforced.

What hasn't changed is mass marketing. The market still rules us more than we rule it. Karl Marx, the Communist, called organized religion "the opiate of the masses." In today's United States, shopping is the opiate of the masses. The advertising and marketing machine that powers the US and world economies is in full control of humanity. Studies have shown that television shuts down the questioning side of our brains.

We are told that we are free to choose. Nothing is forcing us to trade spiritual transcendence for material transcendence. This is a pat answer that maintains ignorance. Freedom of choice requires full knowledge. Our public is not fully educated in or paying attention to the conditioning that's at work. The media are not held responsible for instilling the idea that accumulating material goods can fulfill our need for transcendence.

When a public figure does object to spiritually oppressive messages in the media, he or she is denounced for inhibiting "free speech." A high-profile example of this in recent history was when Tipper Gore took on the music industry in the mid-1980s. Gore demanded packaging labels that would identify violent and/or explicit content. Gore won, and labels have become common not only on music packaging but also on computer games and television shows. The vilification and derision that Tipper Gore endured to achieve this victory resonates to this day. My teenagers don't know Tipper Gore's name, but they deride the idea of labeling and snicker at the concept that the ideas they listen to and interact with directly alter their consciousness.

Public voices instill this derision. Derision of all things that are in harmony with the Light is the subtle subtext of our young people's media. Our children are manipulated into a state of misplaced righteousness that permeates their attitudes as they roam the shopping malls.

Science has shown us that conditioning is indeed a force to be reckoned with. If we hear something enough, we believe it. Things that shock and repulse us when first experienced have no shock effect after repeated viewing. Our essential humanity disappears if an authority tells us he or she will take the responsibility for anything that happens as a result of what we do.[68] The balance of good and evil is a fragile thing.

The media are the parental power of our "village." The media hold the reins of our Messianic power. Pay attention. The law of the land is still that We the People own the airwaves. It is up to you and me to hold the media responsible for the ideas and motivations they instill.

The need to free ourselves from the impulse to seek transcendence via material purchases was made evident to me in the spring of 2006. I attended a library story time at the Las Virgenes Library in Agoura Hills, California, with my four year old daughter Mia. The librarian was reading a book about what moms do. It was a politically correct book with moms who fly airplanes and moms who build buildings. The children all quietly listened until the page showed moms who shop. The group exploded with animated recognition.

It is not, of course, just moms. Men are equally driven to shop for the newest car, cell phone, computer, and television. The popular saying "He who dies with the most toys wins" reflects my point.

Our frequencies are upside down. Our quest for Money Power is empty and corrupt.

The conditioning that instills the idea that the products we buy are essential to our being drives our children to kill each other over sneakers, cell phones, and iPods.

Transcendence must be attained; our genes demand it. Attaining higher consciousness with material things is not possible, but the messages we receive from the media and marketing forces say otherwise. No money gained or spent will ever meet our need for higher consciousness, but we keep spending and spending. We are driven with desire. Most of us are not even conscious of what it is we desire.

The drive is so strong that much of our spending is done on credit, and this credit makes us slaves to banks and corporations. Our society and market are designed to harness our spirits. Our families, oppressed by the overwhelming pressure to conform, are channeling all reflections of the Light to a perpetually debt-based profit machine.

The ninth Absolute is that we will receive all that we ask for. In dealing with this Absolute, we must understand that asking for what we need versus what we want is essentially the difference between good and evil. Oversimplification of this idea is to say living for what you need materially is good and living for what you want materially is evil. The ideal balance is having all that we need and not wanting anything else.

Honoring need over want is how we stay balanced and one with the Light. This Absolute is consistently denigrated in our society. We need food, shelter, and clothing. We need education and tools for working. We need our health. Everything else is a want.

Need fulfillment brings deep and lasting joy. Want fulfillment brings a momentary thrill, a thrill that's quickly replaced with yet another want. When we seek what we do not need, we find ourselves always seeking and never finding.

Spiritual needs are something else. They include love, happiness, and unconditional acceptance. Spiritual needs are fulfilled within us. Our spiritual need, our emotional health, is met by exercising our connections with all other life in the world. How we act and treat the world results in how the world acts and treats us. If you need and want love, you need to give love. Happiness is a choice. Unconditional acceptance is a choice. Happiness and unconditional acceptance don't just happen to you: you realize them. Realizing that love and joy come from inside you is what raising consciousness is all about. This is what finding your inner Messiah means. Realizing your power from within is how you become a Messiah.

In the realm created by the US corporate marketing machine, owning material products is perceived as spiritual ascendance. Advertising manufactures a powerful sense of deprivation in us. An underlying spirit of never having all that we need permeates our existence. We all have more clothes, more house, and more food than we need. This excess in our lives magnifies our sense of lack and diminishes our awareness of our own inner power.

The battle lines have been drawn. Economic growth requires working for money and buying in excess of need. Spiritual growth requires families to find time to communicate with each other and to do work that doesn't pay money. With the overwhelming media and political support for the way money works today, economic growth is winning.

Most of us choose the easiest way to survive. We get the job that leaves us no time for anything else. We rely on the message that all our needs will be fulfilled by buying what we want. This false need fulfillment has driven the rise of pharmaceutical companies. We can now buy medications that can stimulate our brain chemistry to produce the emotions we would be producing for ourselves if our minds and bodies were spiritually engaged instead of materially engaged.

Medications are being used to replace the work of climbing the Tree of Life. The "village oppression" of our society leads us to attempt to replace the spiritual transcendence we must have with vain material possessions or chemical simulations. How can we ever believe that any chemical could substitute for the ascendant frequencies of the Light that come with full human interactions and the mastery of our own lives? The scariest thing about such chemicals is that long-term use can induce irreversible apathy. Selective serotonin reuptake inhibitors (SSRIs), the meds that are used to treat depression, have been shown to induce irreversible apathy.[69]

Apathy is a condition in which you have no sense of or compassion for other people's feelings. We have meds that will simulate the stimulation that comes with connecting to the Light through others. These same meds destroy our ability to perceive others' feelings of connection to the Light. Pay attention to that! Society has always had trouble honoring mankind's oneness. Society is now on the path of destroying mankind's ability to even perceive oneness.

We fear that we will not survive if we do not conform. Fear is an undercurrent that kids in the high schools discuss. Everyone is afraid: afraid of being wrong, doing wrong, attending the wrong school, living in the wrong place, losing jobs, losing money, losing their homes. To young people, all adults live in fear. We do. We fear being an "other." Others are homeless. Others do not get the higher paying jobs. Others cannot pay their bills. Others go to inferior schools and lose their families to mental illness.

The stress of ensuring that we're not an "other" is overwhelming. Conforming results in stress and pain that we accept as the price we must pay to support ourselves. We have to let conforming go and see it for what it is, Money Power oppression.

Our families are shattering under the material burden our country's Money Power operations have instilled in society. Family members who can get with the program, follow the script, keep a stiff upper lip, and stuff their feelings to get through the day get the pat on the back and the rewards. Family members who own the pain, lash out, and/or opt out are the "others." We give them drugs; we try discipline; we do all that we can do. If we fail to enforce conformity, then we ostracize them. There are record numbers of "throwaway kids" in the United States.

Too many parents follow authority blindly. It is not in the public authority's interest to have freethinkers at large. The public authority's interest is in compliance. We insist that our children need to go to college, get a good job, and buy a house. Yet there are other ways to create a good life. Parents and We the People as a whole have to stand for freethinking. To live in honor of the Absolutes is to be a freethinker. To follow authorities without question is dishonor in the Light. That each of us is an autonomous reflector of the Light is the second Absolute. Acting and thinking without questioning authority undermines our own power to reflect the Light

Individuals need autonomy to stay healthy. Parents have the power to empower their children. Parents have to wake up, pay attention, and free themselves from the terror that is instilled by the Money Power. We have to recognize our oppressions and own our own fear to stop oppressing our children. If Jesus were your sibling or child, would he be able to perform miracles at your house? Would Jesus be able to perform miracles in your village?

CHAPTER 6

Right Livelihood Makes Us Magicians

Free Bird

Finding your right livelihood and doing it is exercising freedom. Right livelihood takes you to the place where your heart sings and you can belt out that you are free as a bird, just like Lynyrd Skynyrd in 1973 with the song "Free Bird."[70] Working in your right livelihood ends self-oppression. Working in your right livelihood means you do not have to conform, you do not have to fear; you are doing just what you would be doing, getting paid or not.

Most people who follow their true paths have to fight, disagree, and disappoint people to do it. The people who are disagreeing and being disappointed are completely ignorant of the fact that they are actually practicing the worst kind of black magic: the interference in another person's individuality and mental independence. To quote Manly P Hall, "The white magician seeks to gain control over himself. The black magician seeks to obtain control over others."[71] No matter how altruistic a person thinks he or she is, to interfere with a person's mental autonomy is to practice black magic.

When we are doing the work we are born to do, our pursuit of happiness is in full swing. We've mastered the first three Absolutes. We've found our purpose. The fifth Absolute, change, becomes the creative force with which we work instead of a force we have to fight. Working in our right livelihood means we are in a place from which we can begin to be aware and awake to the paths of the Light and be of service. Loving our work, being awake and aware, and living a life that honors the Absolutes is what it really means to "turn out right."

In esoteric ethics, there are three essential occupations for people who have turned out right, who have become white magicians, fully awake and wielding their full power.[72] The type of livelihood is extraneous to these occupations. Right livelihood shifts and changes according to need. The need to master these three occupations never changes. They are refinement of what it means to pay attention. The three occupations are the ways in which we practice paying attention. The first occupation is service; the second is study, and the third is meditation.

The occupation of service requires being mindful of every moment, thought, and action. Being as fully mindful as possible enables you to consciously reflect the Light on its Absolute frequencies. To be of service is to be dedicated to raising humanity's frequencies to harmonious balance with the Light. Every interaction with life on earth involves bringing the frequencies of the interaction up or down.

To begin service as a white magician, the only change required in your daily existence is to consciously choose to be on the frequency of the Light. To do so means to consciously honor the Absolutes in all of our interactions. Service as a white magician means maintaining a state of mind that not only chooses Light for one's self but also influences others to choose the Light.

The occupation of study requires you to know what is going on in your community, your world, your government. Any formation of human energy that is tapping your power has to be accountable to you if you are of service. A Magician, a Messiah, must always be learning and growing in mastery of the areas of life that draw you to investigation and further inquiry. You cannot be an effective Messiah if you are ignorant.

You cannot be one with the Light if you don't "know."

The occupation of meditation requires you to find time to connect to the "knowing." Quiet the noise in your mind every day and discern what your inner voice is telling you, what you need to attend to, what is important, what is not. Find time to listen to your breath and achieve a silent being. Tune in.

Of course, you can't spend all your time with your mind on esoteric concepts. The frequency of the Light, the joy, is hard to hang onto as we scratch and claw to make a living. Right livelihood is important. Not one of us will live long on this earth if we don't do the work necessary to ensure our physical survival. At the same time, not one of us will transcend to higher consciousness without service, study and meditation.

Service isn't isolated duty in a soup kitchen on Thanksgiving or a large donation to your favorite charity or regular participation in fund-raising efforts or volunteering for your favorite church group. So many of us go through these paces, then we turn around and spend the rest of our time beating the competition. Service in spiritual teachings means that every moment of your living existence is dedicated to harmonizing every living thing around you with the Light. Everything is personal.

Psychiatrist M. Scott Peck tells a story in one of his *Road Less Traveled* books that demonstrates service in the true spiritual sense. He boards a crowded bus in New York City during rush hour. Traffic is jammed. People are late. The bus driver greets him with a friendly warm welcome and does the same to all who board the bus. The driver continues to speak about the sights as they travel down the traffic-jammed roads. He comments positively on people and things observed and he says fond, pleasant farewells to passengers who depart.

Peck observed that each and every passenger's mood lifted and expression softened. Glances of recognition and shared enjoyment developed, even from the most stressed-out, seemingly unhappy passengers. That bus driver was harmonizing his piece of our existence. He was doing the work of the white magician. He was fighting evil in the only way ever successful, harmonizing it to the tune of the knowing.

Was driving a bus this man's right livelihood? Was he born to drive a bus? I don't know. Right livelihood is different for every one of us, but being of service remains the same for every one of us. Service is attitude, not livelihood, not action. Service in the Light is to transmit an attitude of joy and unconditional love. Right livelihood helps but does not guarantee right service. It's easier to maintain the right attitude when we're doing what we "know" is the right work for us to be doing.

My understanding of how to figure out what this work is came from Sister Ann Dwyer, my seventh-grade English teacher at Saint Gabriel's school in Stamford, Connecticut. She caught me one day at the end of a class period in shock because the time was gone. She held my attention on that realization and told me that that was what I needed to seek out in life: work that makes time disappear for me. What this work is may change over our lifetime, or it may stay the same. We are all different.

Finding the work that takes us out of time gives us a taste of transcendence. We do this kind of work because we love it; it is our personal reflection of the Light and it inspires. Such work enlightens us and in return enlightens others. Right livelihood is the work we would do even if we didn't get paid for it. We do this work despite the fact that there is no money in return. When our work brings us joy, we cannot help but be of service to others because we are on the right frequency needed to be of service. Best of all, the beauty of the forces at work is that the money will come.

Choosing a life of service doesn't mean you can't get rich servicing the needs of humanity. Study can include defining society's needs and fulfilling them. In 1849, Levi Strauss made denim trousers for California's gold miners who needed pants that wouldn't wear out in one day of mining. He saw a need; he filled that need. What happened to Levi Strauss and what he did with his Fortune I can't say. I can tell you that Fortune is a midlevel path on the lefthand column on the Tree of Life. To experience it, you must master the sixth Absolute: the path of the human power to create. This path is often referred to as the "Wheel of Fortune" path because fortunes come and go.

Being in tune with the Light does not mean we can't be wealthy. The infinite doesn't care if we are wealthy or not; it doesn't care about us personally at all. We are infinitesimal parts of the whole. The laws that govern the whole are set and impersonal. All the Infinite responds to is the energy we produce, the frequency this energy is on, and its positive or negative charge. What matters is what we do with the wealth we accumulate.

It's interesting how quickly our paths can change from white to black. It's the rare individual who remains unattached to material wealth and dedicated to service. It is a rare person who is able to be free enough to even get out of the "black" from the day of his birth because of his intimate interface and dependency on family.

From day one in life, we base our choice to be constructive or destructive on the reflections of others in our intimate circle. We want our intimates to reflect love for us. We want what they want; we want to please. We are constant seekers of love and approval. Ironically, many of us attract the exact opposite by not doing what we need to do for ourselves. If our focus is on what we think is wrong with us, or on what we have or do not have, or on how we look and how we compare to other people, we are wallowing in the "mud." In the mud, our time is spent figuring out how to please people and meet expectations, often wanting to control others in the process. Our time should be spent building our self-control and discovering our individual talents and skills and excelling in them. When we build our selves into full realization and stay out of the mud, love, approval, and joy come to us without having to ask for them.

CHAPTER 7
Getting Out Of The Mud

Forever Young

I don't know if it is possible to fully eradicate internalized oppression. I haven't. I am now better able to recognize the internalized oppressions at work in my interactions. I have also learned that the way to eradicate the patterns is to talk about them, cry about them, and recognize them.

Conversation is more than an art form; it is a healing tool. Our lives can be changed just by having people who are sincerely interested in us, who stay attentive and relaxed while listening to us and who do not judge us. Bob Dylan prescribed spiritual truth in his song, *Forever Young.* His lyrics express the hope that you will do for others and let others do for you.[73] Discharging distress through doing for others and by letting others do for us adds years to our lives. Conversation with a nonjudgmental, unconditionally accepting intimate is medicine that heals the ills of our world. Being stress free is a prescription for staying forever young.

Our families are supposed to provide this medicine for us. The family tree is our first full reflection of the Tree of Life. But the refractions and distortions that occur because of parental oppression can create generational patterns that become so ingrained that many of us think the family ideal is some "myth" invented to further oppress us. The refraction in families is so bad that a large segment of our population thinks the Light doesn't exist.

Our families are not conscious of what it means to love unconditionally. The accepted tempo in society today leaves us without the resources to "be there" for each other. The oppressions that are part of being in our families make full connections with each other impossible. Talking about them within the family triggers the conditioned refractions and more distress. Unconditional, nonjudgmental listening in families is often impossible without outside help.

Early Christians knew that unconditional listening was required to achieve transcendence. I believe the root reason for the Roman Catholic sacrament of confession is to discharge distress and clear refractions of the Light from our consciousness to better reflect the Light. The

Catholic dogma about the sacrament of confession is that it is for the forgiveness of sins. Sin is another word for refraction of the Light. Forgiveness is the same as unconditional acceptance. Our minds are like prisms, and the refractions of the Light have to be realigned to become reflections of the Light as we find our way up to higher consciousness.

When you have someone to listen to you unconditionally, without judgment, someone who knows you are good and helps you "realign" your pain and confusion, you heal. You maintain and/or regain your intelligence.

Today, for many people, the idea of a priest as someone you can trust and confide in has been lost, just as the idea of family members being people you can trust and confide in has been lost. Today, therapists are paid to fill this need, but they are not unconditional in acceptance of clients. You have to have the money for the service.

The norm in the United States today is not very attractive. We are failing to take personal responsibility for maintaining honor-bound, unconditional relationships. It is so much easier to isolate and numb out: blame society, politicians, and government; shop; watch TV; eat; get high; and live vicariously through the celebrity-of-the-moment's mistakes and successes. We don't want to address our own oppressions, external or internal. We fear what it might mean to work through the pain and the shame to reveal our inner good, to pursue self-realization and to take responsibility for our world. By not facing this fear, we choose to practice black magic.

Ironically, anyone who has experienced the work of recognizing unresolved pain and internalized oppressions via meditation or any of the infinite number of mental and physical therapy options available will tell you that the hardest part is just getting started. We fear finding out that we are not good. This fear is unfounded. We are all good. No refraction on earth, no sin on earth, can take away our goodness. Nothing can take away our power to be full reflections of the Light. I learned this the hard way.

My marriage was filled with lies and unresolved pain from the past. Twelve years of denying the importance of this truth made it so that I couldn't see clearly through my fear and pain to give anyone good attention. My conditioning kept me silent when my marriage became intolerable. My conditioning kept me silent when I needed help as a full-time mom.

As much as I had rejected my early religious training that dictated martyrdom in womanhood, I bought into the myth of the supermom and perfect wife. I believed in the marriage vows. The stress of living up to the myth and the vows and the suppression of emotional pain to keep up the façade of perfection was killing me. Once I realized that I was dying, once I realized there was no honor in my marriage, then I felt free to speak out. Revealing my pain and distress was the scariest thing I have ever done in my life. Finding that I was still good was overwhelming for me. Realizing that all is good, including my ex-husband, is empowerment.

Paying attention involves becoming aware of personal behavior that indicates we have had a disconnect in attention. Paying attention to disconnects in attention seems like a paradox, but once you start you will see it isn't.

When past distress is triggered, we disconnect from the present. When a disconnect happens, our attention is not in the moment. In retrospect, we can recognize disconnect patterns because there will be blanks in our recall of moments and conversations. Putting attention on those blanks, putting attention on what triggered the disconnect, and then talking it out will raise your frequencies. You can start by talking to trees, plants, photographs. You don't even have to work with another human being. Tree hugging has become very popular in the northwest

United States. Trees are even more unconditionally accepting of us than dogs are. Joking aside, just getting started is the hardest part.

The work of service is a conscious choice in approaching human interactions. To be of service is to be conscious of the emotional frequencies you are affecting in the people with whom you come in contact. The Light operates on the frequency of love and unconditional acceptance. The Light connects us all. Consciously looking for and finding that connection in every interaction is to do the work of service. You cannot go around being unnaturally joyous at all times, that would be false service. You can be unconditionally accepting and respectfully pleasant to everyone with whom you come in contact. You can put a "check" on your own distresses when interacting with others. You can open yourself up to experiencing the Light with everyone you meet.

We are all good. We all deserve to have unconditional love and acceptance in family and in our "village." We all deserve to live surrounded by loved ones who support us without judgment. We all deserve to be part of a village that trusts us and operates on the premise that we are good.

First, we must also be unconditionally accepting of our loved ones and all "others." With unconditional acceptance, there are no "others."

With unconditional acceptance we are all human beings in the full spectrum of the Light striving to achieve their right livelihoods and to be of service. All is good.

CHAPTER 8
The Doors Of Perception

Break on Through (to the Other Side)

We raise our children to respect authority, obey police officers, and get out of the way when these authorities have to get their jobs done. We have all been conditioned to give up our authority to allow authorities who work for the good of all to get their jobs done. This conditioning is both good and evil. This conditioning has to be constantly questioned and constantly paid attention to because it enables corruption to flourish. We have to always look at all sides of every perception of our reality.

Alternative perceptions of reality are required if we are to pay full attention and achieve Messianic power. I would be remiss if I did not bring up sex, drugs, and rock 'n' roll and the role they play in our discovering wholeness.

We forget that Jim Morrison's acid-induced flailing on the stage in his performances of the song "Break on Through" was a continuance of experiments begun by the respected author Aldous Huxley. In 1954 Huxley documented his hallucinogenic experience under the influence of peyote in *The Doors of Perception,* in 1954.[74] Drug-induced alternative awareness was a legitimate exploration when first introduced to society. In fact, it still is. According to an article by John Cloud in *Time* in April 2007, two top medical journals, the *Archives of General Psychiatry* and the *Journal of Clinical Psychiatry,* recently report clear benefit from use of psychedelics in treatment of mental illness.[75]

Mental illness is a direct result of self-perceived powerlessness. Drugs open new "doors" in the pathways of perception in our brain. Drugs can help us realize our own power. Drugs help us pay attention. Drugs can not make us whole.

Drugs used to treat "attention issues" are so common today that family doctors, not psychiatrists, are writing the prescriptions. "Attention issues" is the catchall diagnosis for children who cannot sit still and attend to the work they are given to do in school. Adults are also being diagnosed with attention issues. Attention issues run in families. Attention issues are causing problems in schools and in the workplace. We are an attention-deficit society. We are wholeness deficient.

Stimulants help us pay attention. Constant one-on-one attention has shown equally successful results. Doctors commonly convince parents to give children stimulants because schools and parents do not have time to oversee constant one-on-one attention. The stimulants fill a need the children may try to fill themselves later with illegal drugs. The illegal drug trade in this nation thrives on customers who are self-medicating attention issues. We are drugging, both legally and illegally, to fulfill our need for one-on-one stimulation. Pay attention to that!

Corruption is a multilayered truth that we do not like to admit. Corruption, a departure from what is pure and correct, is the norm in the United States today. How the corruption has taken root has been portrayed in countless books and movies that document organized crime figures with government and corporate ties. Why the corruption is maintained is an unspoken question that just hangs over society.

The answer came to me through an unexpected source. I was reading Eustace Mullins' *The Secrets of the Federal Reserve,* originally published in 1952.[76] The facts he lays out are hard to believe even today. Countless other authors confirm Mullins' information and concur with his views. Even more complex and involved Money

Power organizations, central banks, and councils have developed since 1952.

Mullins details how a group of international bankers secretly met on Jekyll Island, Georgia, in 1910 and drafted the Federal Reserve Act to gain control of the money and credit of the American people. With the Federal Reserve banks firmly in their control, these same bankers triumphed with "mind games." Propaganda and manipulation of public figures were successfully used to implement an international debt-based monetary system. The workings of these "mind games launched World War I, caused the Great Depression, and financed the Russian Revolution, the Soviet Union and even Hitler's rise to power.

This book was suppressed in the United States. When Mullins' book was published in 1952, public controversy, derision and misinformation created a lot of "noise" about its message. Some of the "noise" included Mullins' misguided anti-Semitism.

I deduce the true motivation behind the bankers' evil "mind games" to be straightforward profitable business. The bankers involved are businessmen. They are not of one nationality, one race, or one religion. The facts behind the formation of the Federal Reserve as revealed by

Mullins are accurate. The names he names—the corporations and families that lead the debt-based monetary movement—remain very close to those named in 1952, though Mullins revised and updated the book in 1993. These bankers' and corporate CEOs' motivations can be seen as insidious, but I don't think they are or were. I think they are straightforward operations of a Money Power that adheres to the "might makes right" dictate.

The scale of the heartless dishonor in the corporate and political worlds is too much for people to comprehend; it is easier to dismiss it as untrue. This denial does not change the fact that the Money Powers of the world do not have any personal attachment to We the People. Profit has ruled the operations of the Money Power since the dawn of civilization. We all know this. Just try and talk to a bank about your needs when you are in default: business is business, nothing personal.

The Money Power uses propaganda to ignite emotional righteousness and instill ideology when there is a need to cover up corruption and or restructure the way money works. If people have to starve, die or be addicted to drugs in the coverup or in the restructuring, so be it. I am not condoning this way of thinking. I am reflecting the reality. Men and women in charge of the world's debt-based Money Power adhere to "Might makes right."

Mullins is a diligent researcher and compiler of data. One of the lists in his book reveals how and why drugs are used by the debt-based Money Power. This list comes from another book, *Pawns of the Game* by William Carr. Carr's eerily recognizable list of psychological mandates dates from the 1770's and suggests ways to manipulate public opinion and undermine the reputations of opponents. Methods include:

> the use of alcoholic liquors, drugs, moral corruption, and all vice to systematically corrupt youth of all nations.[77]

The mantra of my youth, "sex, drugs, and rock 'n' roll" reverberates differently when looked at from the perspective of authorities deliberately corrupting us to maintain power. It doesn't take a great leap of the imagination to believe that the drugging of America's youth was a good thing for the authorities in the Vietnam era. Many young people in the 1960s were college-educated and fully aware that Communism was not evil. Authoritarian implementation of population control is the evil at work in all "isms." Keeping youth numb and corrupted in the 1960s and 1970s protected federal authority and control of the economy.

I've known for a long time that the illegal drug trade funds the Money Power's covert operations and this financing structure keeps their operations free of congressional oversight. I just couldn't understand why it was allowed to continue. Now I know. Drugs are kept illegal as a control device. Drugs corrupt the youth. The psychological destruction of youthful opponents provides a classic win-win "drug war."

Our government includes a "czar" in the war on drugs. A czar is a head of state. Within United States borders is an entire drug-based empire with its own economy. This empire is ruled by a government czar waging endless war. War is designed to reconfigure wealth. Within our own country is another country ruled by powers intent on permanently reconfiguring the workings of wealth in the United States.

My favorite teenage boyfriends in the 1970s were caught up in selling drugs. It was an easy way to make money, and the law was "stupid." The real stupidity is the trap these drug laws create for rebellious adolescents who are genetically programmed to fight the "stupidity" and injustice of the world. The Money Power exploits teenage rebellion to control us.

The greatest threat to corruption and unjust authoritarian rule is educated youth operating with full intelligence. Drug and vice laws are psychological traps designed to ensnare rebellious youth in "honey pots" that effectively silence their voices. A "honey pot" is a CIA term for setups that corrupt and destroy opponents. Tell intelligent teenagers they can't do something, and they will do it just to prove us stupid. Add the enticement of fast and easy money, and no wonder our prisons are full of drug offenders. Honor in our relationship to drug use is perverted by authoritarian law.

There is a time and place for emotion-based drug use, according to Dr. John Preston, who has written many important books on psychopharmacology. In his seminars, he illustrates the honorable use of highly addictive drugs for emotional or psychological reasons. Perhaps a person suffers from extreme panic and anxiety attacks whenever flying in an airplane. There can be no argument that long-term therapy can eliminate these attacks. Yet, in a short-term emergency—say, if an immediate family member has died and the patient has to fly across country to attend the funeral—there is nothing wrong with prescribing benzodiazepines for use just before and during the flights. A benzo is a highly addictive tranquilizer.

According to Dr. Preston, addiction does not happen when drugs are taken for the right reasons. Drug control officials will argue that determining "right reasons" is the reason for prescription law. Trained professional oversight ensures honorable drug use. The reality is that no authority—medical, religious, social, or political—can ensure honor in drug use. Honor cannot be ensured in any realm. Individuals alone control their state of honor. The drug user alone "knows."

Paying attention and recovering full intelligence require taking full responsibility for our own mental state. Drug use can undermine attention and intelligence. Drug use can enable attention and recover intelligence. A society that operates with honor ensures the freedom of the individual to "know" what is right or wrong and act accordingly for him/herself. To be "one nation under God" is to be a nation that ensures the freedom of the individual to "know" what is right or wrong and act accordingly for himself or herself.

In the mid-1980s, I lived in a neighborhood in East Los Angeles. On my street there were over twenty young people of Hispanic and Middle Eastern heritage living with their newly immigrated parents. My house was a hangout. I was a full-time mom, and over seven years I got to know these kids. My heart broke as they were sucked into the drug culture when they became teenagers. Their defense for their fall from honor was that the law was stupid, just like my friends when I was a teenager.

I wrote a letter to my congressional representative, Henry Waxman, asking him to support legalization of all drugs so that the ridiculousness of the law could be taken out of the equation in our young people's thought processes. He wrote back that national health issues kept him from supporting legislation that legalized drugs. What a joke that is to me.

My neighborhood crumbled. I moved out after gunshots began to be heard outside my house at night. Our nation has the largest prison population on earth, and one very big reason is drug-related offenses. All this waste is allowed on the pretense of keeping our population healthy.

Drug money laundering is interwoven into our domestic economy. Catherine Austin Fitts served as assistant secretary of housing/federal housing commissioner at the Department of

Housing and Urban Development in the first Bush administration. In 1989 and 1990 she had the distinction of supervising the cleanup of approximately $300 billion of troubled mortgage insurance and mortgage fraud and related savings and loan, Iran-contra and black market budget scandals. Fitts discovered that drug money ran through everything she investigated.

The corruption involved in drug commerce is directly responsible for the destruction of what Fitts calls the "Popsicle Index" in our country. This index is the level of confidence we have that our children can walk to our neighborhood store alone, buy a Popsicle, and then walk back home safely.[78]

Our government covertly protects the illegal influx of drugs into a neighborhood, undermining the honor of the inhabitants. The neighborhood crumbles. People lose their homes or move out. Government labels the neighborhood "blighted," and then redevelopment contractors buy up the properties below market value. The properties are redeveloped with government grants, and then these contractors sell the new properties at great profit. Billions of "black market" dollars are laundered into our economy in this way. Thousands of lives are corrupted and families are destroyed. Authoritarian control is strengthened. The corruption is then used to generate fear that drives us to demand still stronger authoritarian control.

Pay attention to what the children are saying. Recently, I was a substitute teacher for a class of incredibly intelligent eighth-graders in upscale Agoura Hills, California. They disrupted class one day with demands that I give an opinion on whether drugs should be illegal. I was a hero for three minutes when I agreed that all drugs should be legal. I disappointed them when I expressed that my belief is not because I support recreational drug use. My belief is based on the fact that I oppose the police state and prison nation we have become because of the drug laws. I oppose the corruption of our youth and the underground economic workings of our nation because of the drug laws. I told my students to pay attention to the psychology at work and the corruption they are embracing.

Being told not to do something will entice young people to do it. No good comes from recreational drinking and drugging. No good comes from going for the "easy" money. My students could easily identify whom they defied by breaking drug laws. They were less comfortable with focusing on whom they support by using and selling illegal drugs.

Many wrongs would be set right if we legalized drugs. The elimination of the black market economy alone would bring us closer to the Light. The Money Power behind the illegal drug trade would become transparent. Drug users would be released from furtive shame and threat of legal action. The size of our prison system would shrink. A wider scope of drug education that addresses the healthy and the unhealthy emotional and psychological reasons for self-medication would become possible. Freedom and honor would be restored.

Working for the legalization of drugs is an honor-bound stance. Fear, derision, and oppression lurk behind keeping drugs illegal to "protect the public's health." Drugs change the balance of what our minds do. Drugs do not create; they stimulate and or block natural function. Correct human stimulation and activities, more often than not, stimulate and balance our minds better than drugs and with more lasting affect. Laws muddy our understanding. Fear, derision and oppression muddy our intelligence.

Many people discovered alternative perceptions of our connections to all of existence by experimenting with drugs over the last century. I do not condone recreational drug usage, but we need to honor the age-old place in our existence for alternative perception. Alternative perception enables human growth. The Light moves in mysterious ways and we do not know which "doors of perception" will be the most important. That we are all connected is scientific fact. Drug use has revealed insights into this connection.

That We the People are gaining insights into this connection is not good for black magicians. Magicians cannot harness the Light of others if the others can see the Light at work. The Money Power cannot maintain control of a people's money supply if the people can see the workings of the system for what it is. Drugs should be honored, not rejected and shamed. Shame comes from fear. What exactly do our authorities fear? We the People's power is the most obvious answer.

Vibrant perception of the power of the people was reveled in, abused, and then seemingly abandoned by the 1960s revolutionaries, but the new consciousness and perceptions remained. They've been reflected in work that includes *Star Wars* and *The Matrix*. The revolution's seeking spirit can also be found in books like *The Da Vinci Code* by Dan Brown and in the widespread interest in Tibetan Buddhism. Alan Watts's 1957 book, *The Way of Zen*, helped introduce Buddhism to the United States. Watts claims,

"Tibetan Buddhism is Roman Catholicism on acid (LSD)."[79] Ridicule and the stigma of moral weakness that authorities have placed on drug use have suppressed public proclamations of new insights. The popularity of *The Matrix, Star Wars,* and Buddhism reveal that oppression has not obliterated new understanding.

Shame keeps drug adventurers of the past hiding in the shadows for fear of public ostracism. Inducing this shame, I believe, was our authorities' answer to the perception "blowback." Drug use is not the path to the Light, but the Light has made itself known to drug users. The power of our minds is only beginning to be understood. No aspect of discovery should be silenced.

The "highs" we can learn to induce in our brains naturally, without drugs, do not taper off with prolonged practice. In fact, practice increases the high. Smiling secretes endorphins into our brain. Just forcing our face muscles to smile makes us high. The more we smile, the happier we are. The same goes for exercise.

Accomplishment induces highs similar to those of cocaine. Accomplishment is a lasting stimulant. Meditation increases our well-being and can induce hallucinatory experiences. Alternative perceptions are very important to our transcendence. Most accepted perceptions in our society actually lower our consciousness as they reject change. Alternative perceptions inspire change. Embracing change is an Absolute. The Light is the force of creation. Creation is change; paying attention to and honoring change is how we create.

Our ability to create is wrapped up in the same forces that enable us to procreate. Sex and drugs, creation and perception are connected. Honor in sex is a rare thing these days. Mastery of our sexual power is a very profound mastery of our ability to create the world we want. Literal physical power is gained via controlled sexuality. There is no difference between male and female sexual power. Both males and females are equally free to squander power or channel power to affect the world we live in. Both sexes need to pay attention to how we honor sexuality. Neither gender has mastered the realization that sexual energy is power, power that we channel to create. Sex is the power we use to create our very existence.

Sex is guided by the same Absolute that guides our power to create money. Every orgasm we release impacts the rest of our existence. Every dollar we create impacts the rest of our economy. Unhooking sex from honor is the equal to unhooking currencies from a gold standard. Sex without strings is the same as printing money without attached value.

The parallel dishonor of sex and money is used to manipulate us every day. Toothpaste will get you sex; the right car will get you sex; the right jeans will get you sex. I am not calling for dogmatic religious abstinence or rules regarding sexual activity. I am saying that the work expended on sexual attraction, sexual activity, and sexual relationships that do not honor the Absolutes destroys the power we could be channeling into work that would bring us all into the Light. Our sexual power is our fullest reflection of the Light. Rational, honor-bound sex is as normal, healthy, and needed as food and drink. Sexual power used despotically destroys, just as poison in your food and drink destroys.

A conscious psychological paradigm shift to channeling sexual energy into an honorable existence is the path to wielding the full power of creation. When we wield the full power of creation according to the Absolutes, our potentials for self-realization manifest.

Self-destruction is not readily perceived. Like bad diet, dishonorable sexual relations can be a slow death. Sex in advertising, sex on television, and casual sex are shrugged off as the way of the world. Corruption of our sexual power is the way of the world. Pay attention. There is very little honor in the current way of the world.

According to the *Zohar*, an encyclopedia-like set of writings that interpret kabbalah, the whole purpose of connecting to the Light is to perceive our filth and garbage so that we can transform them.[80] Cleansing is the biblical metaphor for transformation.

I prefer using the analogy of noise rather than filth and garbage. I think the terms filth and garbage imply judgment. Judgment has no place in the Light because all is good. Transformation, ascendance into higher consciousness, requires the elimination of noise in our connection to the Light. Paying attention keeps our channels open and free of noise. Dishonor is noise. How we relate to sex and drugs is the key to transforming the noise, in our psychology. Once the noise is cleared, our thinking, our speech, and our actions will reflect the Light and our full potentials will be realized.

The 1960s generation experienced the paradox of sex and drugs. Dishonoring the powers at work in sexual activity and drug use can hold us in captivity, trapped in noise. Honoring the powers at work in sexual activity and drug use can enlighten and free us.

The 1960s generation was on to something very profound with sex, drugs, and rock 'n' roll. The power of creation (sex), perception (drugs), and harmonics (rock 'n' roll) are key to full realization of our selves. Individuals must master these three powers if they want to honor the Absolutes and unite with the Light. Mastering the power of creation is how we manage our work and relationships. Mastering perception is how we pay attention. Mastering harmonics is in every word we speak, every action we take and every thought we have. Mastery always involves honor. Honor is more important than anything else when it comes to realizing any transformation mankind can imagine. Honor is choosing the good of all when making decisions about how to use our power.

Rock 'n' roll was the real force behind the 1960s revolution. Rock 'n' roll music is and was far more than background for horny hippy activity. Rock 'n' roll was a vital force that connected an entire generation in its quest for purpose and meaning. This music inspired a social revolution. The mid-twentieth century was a time of science and rationalism and a time when the youth of this nation took up the cause of free thought and defied the religious and political structures that oppressed us. Sixties youth used rock 'n' roll and civil disobedience to blast a hole in society's hypocrisy and in government authorities' dishonesty.

I'm not talking "trippy" esoteric nonsense when I celebrate the power of rock 'n' roll. I'm talking scientific reality. Science has shown us that we are connected to dimensions we cannot see and that we all have different levels of sensitivity to their existence. There are energies that connect us, move us, and motivate us; energies that we can have power over; and energies that can have power over us. Our personal frequencies contribute to and influence our world. We are musical instruments in the orchestra of life.[81] Everything we do, say, and think adds notes to the symphony that is the force of creation.

The most transformative force in our power is music. Honor in use of this force requires circumspect action and control of oneself. Dishonorable sex and drug use confuses us. Dishonorable sex and drug abuse killed the love and joy in the laughter that new age thinkers enjoyed in the realization of their youth. Dishonor changed the frequencies of rock 'n' roll music. Joy turned to anger.

My own ear-ringing experience of the change in frequencies happened in 1979. My date took me to CBGB's, a club in New York City. The

Plasmatics played that night, and their finale was to chainsaw a fully powered electric guitar in half. We had come a long way from "All You Need is Love." I guess you could say the chainsaw event was a new take on "Great Balls of Fire:"

> You shake my nerves and you rattle my brain...[82]

In 1957, the crowd's laughing response to "Great Balls of Fire" was raw titillation of the creative juices. In 1979, the laughter was raw, but the laughter was jaded and destructive. Raw sexual dishonor raged and the crowd's movements were more like fearful quaking than joyous celebration. Rage against powerlessness was pervasive in the club. Corruption and dishonor had won and degradation was celebrated as inevitable. I went home with a pounding headache and despair on my mind.

The universe operates on the force of attraction. Science calls this attraction gravity. Spiritualists call it the Light. Each of us is part of a harmonic scale of existence. We are attracted to music because music harmonizes the force that binds us together. Sex, money, and drugs, like music, can be used to lift us up to the Light. Sex, money, and drugs, like music, also can be used to block the Light and spur violent and degrading action. The balance is ours to maintain.

No human authority can balance the Light at work in our lives, community, or nation for us without our consent. Question authority. The last thing we want to do is get out of the way so that authorities can do their job without question.

We must pay attention to the workings of public psychology and challenge all public voices we perceive forwarding the "might makes right" dictate. We need to look deeper when a public figure is being subjected to defamation. "Right makes might" adherents are "crucified" on a regular basis in the modern "spin" zone. Freedom only exists if We the People pay attention to the motivations behind all the forces at work in the creation of our existence.

CHAPTER 9
Self-oppression

Mother and Child Reunion

Letting go—recognizing that all is not right with your world or your self—is what transcending through the eighth Absolute is all about. Mastering the eighth Absolute—recognizing that death and birth are the same thing—trips up everyone and everything on the paths of the Light.

Balancing the eighth Absolute is balancing right and wrong. Balancing the eighth Absolute is balancing black and white magic. Balancing the eighth Absolute is the key to successful parenting and the key to successful government. Balancing the eighth Absolute is the key to Messianic consciousness. Letting our wants as parents and as authorities die when they conflict with what is good for our children and the people we affect can be emotionally overwhelming. Imbalance in this mandate is behind just about everything that goes wrong in parenting, communities, and nations.

Resisting change, refusing to let go of what we want as authorities and find alternatives, can provoke feelings of violence. The urge to kill and subjugate others takes over unless we master this Absolute. I often think of letting go as being willing to be naked. The trust we have to place in the Light to let go makes us that vulnerable. At the same time, the sentiment expressed by Paul Simon in the lyrics of his song, "Mother and Child Reunion,"[83] that the reunion is only a moment away, is a perfect insight to how easily balance and interface can be returned to relationships and nations once we do let go of our need to control.

"Getting naked" played a big part in my spiritual transcendence and my relationship with my mother. For decades, I believed the subtext of my unhappiness with my mother was about female oppression, parental oppression, and religious oppression. It was not until after her death that I came to understand that the real oppression blocking our relationship was internalized. My internalized oppression was the blocked me from unconditional acceptance of my mother.

In turn, I have come to realize that the real oppression of freedom that blocks full realization of the ideal that is the United States comes from the internalized oppression of We the People.

Internalized oppression blocks people from fully realizing their authority over the government.

On the personal level, female oppression in the form of "right to work" was not much of a concern with my mother. It was accepted that I might not ever have to support myself. That is what internalized oppression is all about. Internalized oppression is the unconscious acceptance of prescribed roles according to sex and race, etc.

My mother was a realist. Reality is that life is never what you expect it will be. Preparation for circumstances in which I might have to support myself was of paramount importance to my mother. My maternal grandmother was an army nurse who served in both world wars. She continued to work as a registered nurse for her whole working life. Education was the key to liberation in her family. My maternal grandfather's mother died destitute and unable to support her children. My grandfather was stealing bread at a very young age to feed his sisters. I was raised to understand that no matter what happened in life, wars, economic disasters, or natural disasters, my education was the one thing I could not lose.

Grandma grew up on a farm in Missouri. Work was a given in life. Pay was not an issue; survival was. Self-value was. The women in my mother's family were strong and independent.

They didn't need "women's liberation." The struggle I was dealing with, the struggle I could not name, the cause I fought for without knowing what I was fighting for, was freedom from self-oppression, internalized oppression. My belief that my being female somehow prescribed my roles in life was ingrained. Internalized oppression causes frustration and resentment seemingly without cause. I tried to name the cause and, invariably, blamed my mother.

My mother embraced the Messianic aspect of motherhood. I did not understand the eighth Absolute in relation to motherhood. I didn't get that giving up wants in the face of needs raised our consciousness to different spiritual levels. I was subject to the forces in my generation that did not celebrate the Absolute value of parenting and motherhood. I saw my mother as a victim of religious oppression. She happily sacrificed her wants and needs for her husband's and children's. Her mantra was "You do not have sex, get married, and/or have children unless you are ready to take full responsibility for the consequences and dedicate your life to them." My mother's mantra is the very essence of honor.

I did not understand honor then. I did not understand the spiritual truth of my mother's mantra. One of the reasons she loved the Roman

Catholic faith was because of the dogma of the Assumption of the Holy Mother. To me, the idea that both Mary and her Son "rose" to heaven in full physical body and soul was one of those "They are not telling the whole truth," suspicious Church "authority" teachings.

When I understood that in the Messianic consciousness teachings "assume into heaven" means achieving full Messianic "wholeness" was when I also realized what my mom was talking about. Jesus' mother didn't get beamed up into heaven. Mother Mary "rose in consciousness." Mother Mary achieved full reflection of the Light in both body and spirit. By this I mean she reflected the Light in both her material life and her spiritual life. Jesus' mother is credited with revealing that love and joy balanced with anxiety and grief and the relinquishment of power over one's children so that they may achieve their own Messianic consciousness combine to form a vital and revered path to wholeness.

The mother of Jesus achieved ascendance into full Messianic consciousness in this way. She was not a martyr. Messianic consciousness is achieved by letting go of power over our creations. Messianic consciousness is achieved by being an example of what it is to live in honor of the Absolutes.

Neither the motherhood path nor the fatherhood path to full Messianic consciousness is taught. The sacredness of motherhood is taught. But I have found that the religiosity attached to the sacredness of motherhood teachings neglects to clarify the Messianic role of motherhood. As a result, women sacrifice their own needs and wants for their children like martyrs. Achieving Messianic consciousness does not require martyrdom. Sacrificing our needs to do for our children has to be balanced by our children sacrificing to do for us. Our children sacrifice for us first and foremost by letting go of their need for us.

Sacrifice is something you do for yourself. Sacrifice enables your spiritual and material growth. Messianic consciousness can be achieved via parenthood. Sacrifices are required; these sacrifices are for the parent's growth, not the children's. The children have to realize their own growth.

All full-time parents are in a position to channel intense amounts of Messianic power. The Light is in full creative operation on parental frequencies. The balance of love and joy with grief and anxiety provides a path to higher consciousness. To master the parental balance of loving and letting go of control is to master the eighth Absolute and gain entry into all the higher Absolutes.

The religious dogma that motherhood is sacred and a mother must sacrifice for family neglects the mastery of the higher consciousness that comes with this sacred sacrifice. The power gained is not celebrated. The potential for raising one's self to an even higher consciousness following the successful mastery of loving, raising, and letting go of one's children isn't explored. Instead, women are encouraged to sacrifice the need to transcend to wholeness; in return, they expect children to sacrifice their needs and wants and transcendence for them. Ugh.

My mother was fully conscious of the failure of parents to let go when their children were grown. She often shared her insights into this aspect of parenting. Oppression of her children for her gain was not her mode of operation. Honor was. I did not understand the difference.

When I was six or seven years old, I put on a pair of red flannel pajama pants backward by accident. They were an old pair that had belonged to my older brother. The bottom half of a Halloween costume, the red pants were a devil suit with an attached triangle tipped tail. When I realized what I had done and what the tail looked like, I was hysterical with laughter and danced gleefully out to the front of the house to show everyone. I found my mother first. She laughed with me, and in my increased joy, I started twirling the tail around and screaming, "I'm a boy, I'm a boy!" and laughing.

The laughter brought my father into the room and when he took in what we were laughing at, he was furious and ordered me to my room. I was shocked and looked to my mother for support. My mother nodded understandingly but concurred with my father. I went to my room, shamed. A seed of rebellion was planted that day.

A graduate of a Catholic woman's college, Mom married at age twenty-six. She was a no-nonsense realist with a religious discipline that never wavered. By the time I became an adolescent, I was a thorn in her side. It was the 1970s and sexual freedom was the norm. From my perspective, my mother was oppressed and repressed and needed to rebel. A neighbor friend once asked her to attend a women's liberation meeting, and my mother refused. Her rationale was that if she attended she would probably decide to leave her husband, she did not want to leave her husband, and so she was not going to get involved.

Mom's beliefs about sexuality were evident in the books that I was not allowed to read. She took Jacqueline Susann's book *Valley of the Dolls* away from me after learning its contents. At the same time, she gave me a book by Kathleen E. Woodiwiss titled *Shanna* because a woman at the library recommended it. The romance novels by Woodiwiss include graphic sexual encounters just as Susann's books do, but her characters are always married before they have sex, not necessarily fully connected on a spiritual level, not in love, but married.

Our conflicting ideals exploded one night when I came in from a date. I had been parked in my date's car for a couple of hours outside the house. When I came into the house, my mother screamed at me and called me a slut. My father and brother were there, and once we all calmed down, the fact that I hadn't been having sex was believed and peace was restored. It was an uneasy peace because I did become sexually active before marriage. Ease wasn't restored until I was married and became a mother myself.

My mother didn't bestow true redemption on me until I had stuck out years of unhappy marriage and proved my self-sacrificing mettle. My emotions about that time are bittersweet. Redemption occurred when my father attempted to suggest that I rethink my divorce just before it was final. Mom startled all of us by telling him to shut up. As far as she was concerned, I was "a saint" after all that I had been through.

Time stopped for me in that moment. Mom never used the term "saint" lightly. She especially didn't apply it to someone who was acting in direct defiance of the Church's teachings. Mom's perspective had changed. She was dying of gallbladder cancer and life was too short. Martyrdom and motherhood had been completely divorced in her mind.

I moved into my parents' house for the last months of my mother's life. When I arrived, my mother was valiantly carrying on her toiletry alone; her dignity demanded this. She was not comfortable with nudity in front of my father or anyone else. She had a tube implanted in her side to drain bile from a body that no longer could drain on its own. This had her doing a modesty dance with my father. Mom's vulnerability endeared her to me like nothing else could ever do. Her hesitation in asking me to help her bathe was disarming. Suddenly my freethinking attitude that was comfortable with nudity and at ease with sexuality was an asset that provided my mother with full acceptance, a comfort zone that she could rely on.

The final resolution came one day before her bath. We had to call my father in to help with her tubing. By this time my mother could not speak clearly anymore; she communicated with nods and sounds of assent or dissent.

We started, my father and I, to manipulate her clothes in our ritual preservation of her modesty. All of a sudden, Mom stood tall, shoving us away. She caught my eye. Hers were twinkling like only the Irish can twinkle. She shrugged off her gown and let it drop dramatically to the ground. She threw back her head and gave my father such a look of defiance, I had to laugh and applaud. My mother had crossed to the other side; she had joined the rebellion. She was naked!

My father was flabbergasted. To his credit, he chuckled and simply said, "So that's the way it's going to be? Good." We took care of her needs and he left us.

My mother and I had eight weeks of intimacy and understanding that she called a gift from God. I call it full interface with each other and the Light. My mother raised five children and her marriage lasted more than forty-eight years, until her death in 1998.

Over the last weeks of her life, before speaking became difficult for her, my mother spent a lot of time considering any regrets she might have. She repeatedly reviewed her choices. She wondered if she could have done more. She wondered if there were things she might have done for herself. After much reflection, she would always reject the notion and assess that she consciously chose her life. She made careful and studied choices. She was proud of her five children. She was proud of how she conducted her life, no regrets. She never lost faith and she lived at all times according to her belief with honor. She died free.

Mom believed she lived life free too. She consciously chose her life. Mom treated life as an adventure; adversity was something that would pass. Learning was what mattered. Mom had an inquisitive mind. Interest in fully understanding anything and everything she came in contact with was a constant in her life. Being of service was her way of life.

I supported my mother's dying view of her life lived freely. Her reasoning about her choices made sense. I didn't learn about the power of internalized oppression until after her death. I'm glad, because I would have been a thorn in her side with information about subconscious conditioning. Instead, my mother and I could simply enjoy intimacy without words. Understanding internalized oppression was mine to discover.

My journey to the place where I could be there for my mother for eight weeks dedicated just to her needs was not so free, not so easy. My rebellion inspired by women's liberation was a painful path. I wanted to have it all: motherhood and a full career. The extreme distress caused by fulfilling these desires was not expected. The reason parents kill their own children is related to the kind of personal distress I experienced in my children's younger years.

We only hear about the sensational cases like the Texas woman who systematically drowned her five children in the bathtub while her husband was at work or the young mother who drove her car into a lake, drowning her two toddlers strapped in the backseat. Less publicized cases occur every day. Observers shake their heads in wonder; no one can understand how anyone can do such a thing to his or her own child. I do. Don't tell me you have never heard a parent say, "I could kill my kid!" Yeah, you say, but you claim you would never do it.

The crisis of mother oppression happened for me years before my mother's death. I experienced a momentary flash, a voice in my head in a moment of distress, "Kill the children." This moment shocked me to the core of my soul. Shaking with fear and distress, I immediately reassessed my life and my options. Most important, I had to face the fact that I was overwhelmed by the suppression of my needs. I was allowing external reflections of my lack of success to influence my priorities.

The crisis occurred following a job interview. At the time, I had over nine years of experience in television production. I was a graduate of the American Film Institute's producing program, and I had a lot of personal ambition. I was good at what I did.

I also had and have a strong belief that children ages one through six require a full-time loving parent at home. Grandparents and immediate family can buffer this need, as can a great hired caregiver. But my husband and I did not have such luxuries to fall back on. No family lived nearby, and the cost of good quality childcare exceeded the monetary benefit my working would bring in. I stayed home for five years.

I started looking for a re-entry job when the two children were both in full-time Montessori school. My marriage, as I already stated, was killing me, and I had the attitude that I was losing my intelligence, my self. It was obvious to me that full-time mothering was not making me the best mother to my children. Being in the house is not the same as being there for them.

A very professional woman at an entertainment employment agency was impressed with me. She felt that there would be no problem finding me a job. I felt good; I was going to re-enter the work I loved, maybe even at a production company I really admired.

Then I said, "The only thing is, I will have to be able to pick my children up by six o'clock every evening."

"That will not be acceptable," the interviewer answered. "You know how this business is. The hours go long. You'll be required to work late according to company needs."

"I know how it can be. My husband's an editor. He already works late most nights," I said. "I can be available from six in the morning until six at night. My children's school closes at six. I have to be there by then."

The interview went downhill from there. There was no way anyone would accept time stipulations in the entertainment business. I was advised to hire a nanny or an elderly woman from my church, someone who could pick my children up and feed them dinner and bathe them for me every evening. To my utter incredulity, my interviewer assured me that I would get the quality time with my children by tucking them into bed at night. I thanked the woman, asked her to keep me in mind should something part-time come up, and left.

As I exited the building on Sunset Boulevard, a huge billboard leered at me. A beautiful model with a baby at her breast was advertising some obscure product and bold letters above her read: "A CHILD, THE ULTIMATE PET." I was in emotional turmoil, a mess of outrage and confusion.

As I drove over Coldwater Canyon, the idea to kill my children flashed into my mind. I say flashed. The shock caused me to pull over to the side of the road and have an immediate realignment of thought.

I chose to have my children; they are what life is all about. I organized my options, planned alternate paths of action for myself, and rediscovered hope.

When I got home, I called my friend Jody, also a full-time mom, and confessed to her what I couldn't confess to my husband. We discussed it. She hadn't ever reached that level of desperation, but she could see the reasons. She assured me that what really counted was that I rejected the thought as quickly as I had it.

I suggested that maybe some good could come of it; I could use the crisis as a "Movie of the Week" plot. We laughed when Jody admitted she just watched something similar. Based on a true story, the woman in the movie shot her children because she felt the man she loved rejected her because of them.

I am not horrified when I hear about parents killing their children. I fully understand the deep pain of parental oppression, mother oppression. What I am really upset about is the lack of ready resources for parents. There is a societal collusion in this oppression. Society is in denial. We do not own what we are doing to ourselves. We hear about the need for affordable day care; we hear about the need for more opportunities for women; we hear about the need for family-friendly jobs. The issue isn't about feminism, and it isn't about some kind of undeserved luxury. It is about life. A child's life and a parent's life are both at stake.

The rage that fueled the feminist revolution was justified, but the solution is not pat. The ploy to replace our need for personal transcendence with shopping has been so successful because internalized oppression is not easy to divine. Denial and avoidance are easier. The "women's liberation" movement that formed my attitudes in the 1970s was a lie. The media blitz on bra burning and deriding male machismo was another form of social oppression and spiritual degradation for whole families.

If anyone needed liberation in the 1970s, it was men. They were more disengaged from the Light their families offered. Men need to be freed from the internalized oppression that locks them into the role of a selfless provider who feels no pain and has no emotional needs. Instead, with "women's liberation," women entered into the same material transcendence model that had already disengaged men from the family. Engagement requires mastery of the eighth Absolute.

The eighth Absolute, dying to restore life, is a valid requirement of good parenting. The paths that lead to Messianic consciousness require us to let go of our material attachments to realize work we really need to do. A family's needs require all members to let some wants die. "Healthy family" means that not all the wants that die are the parents'. Service, the constructive work of harmonizing humanity, starts with a healthy family. These Absolutes at no time require full sacrifice of one's own power, one's own being. If they did, we would not be able to do the work for lack of power.

Religious, societal, and familial forms of oppression are responsible for behavior patterns that oppress the very Light we need to be good mothers, fathers, lovers, men, and women. Without self-realization, there can be no connection to the Light; there can be no joy to give.

Clothes are a metaphor for blocks on our power. Oppression correlates to the clothes that Adam and Eve put on when they were ejected from the biblical Garden of Eden. The stress of survival ensures that the oppression continues, because it interferes with our full intelligence. Without full intelligence we cannot recognize internalized oppression and we cannot have healthy families.

Getting free of oppression is not easy. Getting "naked" is not easy. But the alternative is not worthy of the Light. Choosing clothes, cars, TV, and money as material forms of transcendence is spiritual death. Choosing to stay clothed in oppressed ignorance is to deny the realization of the eighth Absolute. Denial leads to endless shopping. Denial leads to poor health and physical death. Denial leads to violence. Our spirits are dying, and our own internalized parental oppression is allowing spiritual death to spread to generation after generation. Internalized oppression has to stop. We need to get naked.

Getting naked makes me think of streakers, the naked protesters who raced across America's baseball fields and the stages of nationally televised award shows. Getting naked brings to mind Woodstock and Joni Mitchell's lyrics calling us back to the garden. Getting back to the garden. Getting back to standing proud in our nakedness. Getting back to the unconditional Tree of Life teachings. Getting back to the Absolutes. Getting back to We the People being the government of the United States. Getting back to placing honor above all else. This is the way to the promised land.

It's no accident that Woodstock happened in the United States. Life in the United States of America is the closest to Absolute existence mankind has managed so far. The United States of America is founded on the Absolutes. Existence in the biblical Garden and the Promised Land is to live in full honor of the Absolutes.

Full realization of this reality is ours if and when each and every one of us does the work to align ourselves with the Absolutes and, in turn, demands that our nation as a whole does the same. Our honor is reflected in our nation's honor and, in turn, our nation's honor is reflected in the world's honor. The only thing in our way to realizing full ascendance to Messianic consciousness and all that mankind holds as ideal is ourselves, our own internalized oppressions.

CHAPTER 10
The Absolute USA

The Star-Spangled Banner

"Oh, say does that star-spangled banner yet wave, O'er the land of the free and the home of the brave?"[84] The banner still waves, but is the United States still the land of the free and the home of the brave? The ability to say yes to this question is hanging by a thread. Homeland security actions taken in response to the "War on Terror" threaten our freedom. Fear mongering is standard political rhetoric in the home of the "brave" today. Shirking our duty as Messiahs has allowed the War on Terror to escalate to the point that our land is losing its identity. Shirking duty is much the same as internalized oppression.

Internalized oppression as a mother means I am not becoming the whole person I need to become because I've internalized the idea that as a mother I have to give up my personal growth. Internalized oppression as a US citizen plays out in my not paying attention to authorities and forces at work in my government because I have accepted that they are outside of my control. I have spent years shrugging off personal responsibility for government oversight. I would say, "I have enough to worry about taking care of my own life." Sound familiar?

The rise of George W. Bush has forced me to wake up and pay attention to the state of our union. The election of 2000 was my first alert. Watching television on election night, I heard that Al Gore had won Florida. I watched a broadcast of the Bush family standing up and leaving a restaurant. Their body language was very determined. They took a limousine to the home of Jeb Bush, the Florida governor. I watched the backs of this family as they entered the mansion and I "knew" they were going to do something.

Just a few hours later my suspicion was confirmed. Florida switched and following much controversy George W. Bush was named our new president-elect.

The "knowing" is a very personal experience, not one that I usually share with people. This time, I could not help discussing my experience and suspicions. Invariably, my "knowing" was confirmed by others in the same frame of mind. Election inconsistencies, incompletely punched chads, and computer programs that switch votes are common knowledge to those who have been paying attention to this issue. Then came the incomprehensible events of 9/11 and continued inconsistencies in our election process in 2004. Dishonor permeated my perception of the United States.

I became driven to discover what was really going on in our nation. I began to do research. I dove into our history in the Middle East. I began to read everything I could find that was written on 9/11. One discovery would lead to another, and the best activists' work pointed me to historical books and writings. I became somewhat manic in my immersion into this research.

The presidential claims of entering into a War on Evil spurred me on. I was driven to get to the naked state of our nation. I wanted to find exactly what was upside down in the workings of our nation in honoring the Absolutes.

What I found first and foremost is that the United States is literally founded on principles that honor the Absolutes. I mean literally. I was surprised and proud as a citizen to find literal parallels. The Great Seal of the United States of America is a case in point. On the front, we have the bald eagle. Students of symbolism agree that this is a "fire" bird, that this eagle is a conventionalized phoenix.[85] In the mystery schools, the phoenix symbolizes rising again out of the ashes of death. It is a symbol that represents mastery over the eighth Absolute. It makes sense that the original idea was to have a phoenix as our bird. I have also read that Ben Franklin wanted it to be the humble turkey. I get a kick out of that idea, because being humble is also essential to the mastery of the eighth Absolute.

The bald eagle has actually become both a phoenix and a turkey. The bald eagle once was near extinction. With humanity's help, the bald eagle has become a phoenix. The bald eagle survives on dead animals; life doesn't get much humbler than that. The bald eagle still flies proud and inspires thoughts of freedom. The bald eagle is a fitting symbol for our nation.

Even more important, to me is the symbol on the seal's obverse side: the pyramid with the floating capstone with the eye engraved on it. This pyramid symbol is a Magi symbol. The capstone floating above the base represents mankind's higher nature, our Messianic potential. The base of the image represents mankind's worldly nature, our base instincts. The capstone of the pyramid will connect with its base when all of mankind achieves Messianic consciousness. The pyramid will be whole when mankind reaches wholeness.

That our founding fathers saw fit to include the Magi pyramid symbol on our nation's Great Seal leaves me with no doubt that they had every intention of founding a nation based on the Absolutes that lead to Messianic consciousness.

I was also thrilled to discover that the Absolutes as I have translated them from the main paths of kabbalah are directly reflected in the founding documents of the United States of America. The dictates of the Declaration of Independence and the Constitution of the United States combined climb the Tree of Life.

As I systematically worked my way through our founding fathers' documents and written history, the kind of Messianic force we have become began to worry me. As someone who is working on paying attention, full attention, to how my connection to the Light is affecting the world, I want to see confirmation that I lend my power to the Light. As a citizen of the United States, I want to see the Light reflected in the workings of my nation. There can be no doubt the United States has been a shining example to the world. There can also be no doubt that the United States of America has participated in the harnessing of the world for economic gain.

I attempted to discern the points of honor that need attention for us to maintain the United

States' Messianic nature in the Light. This inspired me to locate each Absolute in the Declaration of Independence and in our Constitution. I figured that if I could discern our nation's honor or dishonor in compliance to the Absolutes as dictated in our founding documents, I might be able to make some sense out of what the United States needs to be doing today.

What I have found is enlightening. Both the shining honor of the United States and the dark dishonor of the United States have become clear to me. The way to restoring our Republic to full honor shines brightly when we pay attention to what we are supposed to be. There is nothing wrong with the United States today that can't be put right by honoring what is right in our founding documents.

CHAPTER 11
Revolution Is A US Citizen's Mandate

Born in the U.S.A.

The first five Absolutes are in our Declaration of Independence. What an auspicious beginning for a nation. We are a nation born to be a base for Messianic consciousness.

The story within Bruce Springsteen's song "Born in the U.S.A.," reflects the bizarre reality of what the United States has become.[86] Springsteen sings about the pride of a soldier and serving in the Vietnam War; he sings about being unable to find a job; he sings about being kicked when down. President Ronald Reagan used the chorus of this same song for political campaigning in 1984. Springsteen says in this song, "you spend half your life just covering up." The truth of these words is why Reagan's use of the song worked.

For all the oppression, societal and self-imposed, the roots of the United States are honor bound. Our impulse to cover up is honor bound. Honor bound means we believe the good of all comes first. US citizens can find hope in this fact. We the People resonate to an Absolute spirit. Everything about us that is not Absolute, we cover up and deny because unequal and unjust is not what we believe we are. Dishonorable is not what we want to be.

Hypocrisy to further the well being of all can be acceptable. In the early '80s, my mother sighed that she wished for a little more hypocrisy in the world. Life was more pleasant when the public wore the façade of being in line with the Absolutes. What she meant was that real life is not *The Andy Griffith Show,* but projecting an image more consistent with our ideals reflects honor and keeps us more honor bound.

Portraying ideals as if they are reality can raise our expectations of ourselves. Yet, hypocrisy in who we are as a nation has put us in jeopardy. We have allowed ourselves to become what psychiatrist Scott Peck calls the "People of the Lie," and We the People are in danger of losing our sovereignty. It's a "don't use it, you lose it" situation. We the People are supposed to rule the United States of America, but we don't. We ignore harsh truths. We do not even know truths because of national security secrecy law.

What we do know about assassinations, support for drug cartels, and US-run insurgencies that overthrow other nations' governments is comfortably blacked out of our public psyche. What the Department of Homeland Security might be doing is not part of our perception of supporting liberty for all. This hypocrisy has dishonored the mantle of Messianic power that we wear as citizens of the United States.

The first and second Absolutes are that we are all born with the power to reflect the Light and that we all have equal power to reflect the Light. Both of these Absolutes are found in the words of the Declaration of Independence: "all men are created equal." There can be no doubt that over the last century the women's suffrage and civil rights movements have made great progress in honoring these first two Absolutes in the United States. More people are paying attention to equality and fairness than ever before. Young people today are far more open and accepting of different cultures and ethnicities than the generations before them.

Still, the response to the victims of Hurricane Katrina in New Orleans compared with the past response to victims of hurricane damage in more affluent "white" coastal areas shows us that we still have a long way to go in gaining full honor in this primary Absolute. The fact that the United States has suspended habeas corpus and uses "enhanced interrogation techniques" on terror suspects in direct defiance of our Constitution and the Geneva convention shows that We the People are not paying attention.

The third Absolute says that combining our frequencies to reflect the Light with others on the same frequencies exponentially increases those frequencies. We find this Absolute reflected in the Declaration's words, "governments are instituted among men, deriving their just powers from the consent of the governed."

The consent of the governed is more than just voting. We need to be ever vigilant. Voting, though, is a start. For citizens to exercise full Messianic power, we have to vote. There are those who claim the system is rigged; there are those who say voting is useless. They are right, but citizens must hold officials accountable for inconsistencies and manipulations of the voting system. More important, we have to vote in the first place. Since 1944, only 40 to 55 percent of those eligible typically cast votes in presidential elections. In local elections, the percentage is even lower. This is not good enough. You are one with the Light. You give your power, conscious or not, to those who govern you. Pay attention to whom you give your power.

Not voting gives away your power as much as voting does. Honor is choosing to act for the good of all in the face of forces you cannot control. We cannot control all of humanity. We can vote for the control we believe is best. To have honor, you have to vote. Even if the voting system is being tampered with, even if votes are being flipped, we have to vote. If there is no one for whom you wish to vote, then it is time to start a new party with a candidate you do want to vote for! Overwhelming numbers, full participation cannot be denied. No one can stop We the People from achieving our will when we apply it.

The fourth Absolute is that we all have a purpose. We all have a right livelihood, something that brings us happiness, something that makes us one with the Light. Finding that purpose, finding the Light, is the pursuit of happiness. The fourth Absolute is revealed in the most famous words of our Declaration of Independence, words which tell us that all men: "are endowed by their Creator with certain unalienable rights, that among these are life, liberty and the pursuit of happiness." The pursuit of happiness and honoring the fourth Absolute are the same thing.

The United States has done a good job of protecting our individual right to be and become who and what we choose to be and become. The blocks that exist in society are not insurmountable. Self-oppression is more to blame than any other block in our realization of the fourth Absolute.

The United States was established to maintain our individual right to be free. It is up to us, the citizens, to maintain our freedom. It is up to us to break the chains that bind us. Our founding fathers gave us a republic in which We the People are sovereign; it is up to us to hang on to our reign.

Finally, the fifth Absolute is that change is inevitable and must be allowed to happen according to the dictates of the Light. We find this fifth Absolute reflected in the Declaration's most powerful words:

> whenever any form of government becomes destructive to these ends (the first four Absolutes), it is the right of the people to alter or to abolish it, and to institute new government, laying its foundation on such principles and organizing its powers in such form, as to them shall seem most likely to effect their safety and happiness.

The fifth Absolute is where we take a stand. Our right to impeach our government authorities is one of our most important and necessary rights. We the People are revolutionaries. It is our mandate to pay attention to change at all times. We are to confirm that change is for the good of all. We are to demand change that is for the good of all when it is being denied. Our personal spiritual ascendance and our national wholeness depend on us paying attention and standing at the ready to act in the spirit of the fifth Absolute at all times. Dissent is patriotic.

The Declaration of Independence resonates today with the same power it did in 1776 on the day it was introduced to the world. The Declaration of Independence mirrors the Absolutes that form the base of the Tree of Life. It truly is a sacred document.

I believe, after careful study, that as a nation we can be proud of our record of honor in the maintenance of the first four Absolutes. Even though there is still and always will be work to be done, We the People have maintained the base of the United States with honor. At the same time, the fraying of this honor is becoming evident in our nation's operations behind the War on Terror.

Consider the wording of a bill to establish the "National Commission on the Prevention of Violent Radicalization and Homegrown Terrorism, and for other purposes," bill # S.1959, which under the same title passed in the House as H.R. 1955 with overwhelming bipartisan support and was introduced to the Senate in August of 2007. If this bill passes, the words I just cited from the Declaration will become cause for charging our own with "violent radicalization." Shame on the House for passing this bill in such overwhelming numbers; we can only hope the Senate kills it.

Paying attention scares me. Figuring out what to do is overwhelming. Standing to protect our honor is our dictate as citizens of the United States. We are responsible for constant vigilance over the Absolutes at work in our nation.

It is up to us to pay attention and act in honor of the fifth Absolute if our government fails to maintain freedom and adherence to the dictates of the Light. I look to our Constitution for answers. The Constitution is the tool our founding fathers used to master the higher Absolutes in bringing our nation to form. The Constitution tackles how money is to work in our nation. Money is our magic wand.

CHAPTER 12
Money Changes Everything

Money

The sixth Absolute is that everything we create is sacred. Money is one of our finest creations. The creator God of the Old Testament took special care instructing us how to use money. Pink Floyd in 1973 sang that money was evil and a crime, but don't take a slice of mine.[87] Self-preservation easily overwhelms honor in the face of financial loss. Honor in the money supply is a very difficult to maintain. Our founding fathers worked hard to honor sacred truth in creating the United States of America. Honor in our money supply was a first priority.

In 1786, riots, looting, strikes, unemployment, and rampant bankruptcies shook America. Social unrest was overwhelming. In *The Miracle on Main Street, Saving Yourself and America from Financial Ruin*, F. Tupper Saussy reveals the true cause of that social unrest:

> The history books tell us it was a complicated variety of interrelated things, but reality tells us it was only one: the money issued by the Continental Congress and the States' banking houses was paper that could not be redeemed for gold or silver coin.[88]

Saussy's book is self-published and includes a hard-to-find reprint of the writings of Roger Sherman on this topic. Sherman is the only man to sign all three of the founding documents of the United States of America: the Declaration of Independence, the Articles of Confederation, and the Constitution of the United States. Sherman was the colonial champion of honest money.

We don't hear about Roger Sherman in our American history classrooms because his stance has not been the historical "winner." History's winners write history. Now that I have read Sherman's *A Caveat Against Injustice,* I know we have to resurrect his memory and honor the work of Roger Sherman! He stood for restricting the government's ability to print paper money at will. Today's Federal Reserve prints paper money at will. Sherman's work was dedicated to ensuring that the United States would have an honest money supply. The United States today does not have an honest money supply. We could have one. We are supposed to have one. We the People need to know what one is. We the People need to take action to re-establish one. Revolution over the workings of money is an American mandate.

Modern mainstream historians skate over the monetary aspect of our American Revolution with the summary that the issue was "taxation without representation." We are taught that "taxation without representation" was the cause of the revolution even though Benjamin Franklin is credited with telling us that:

> the colonies would gladly have borne the little tax on tea and other matters had it not been that England took away from the colonies their money, which created unemployment and dissatisfaction. The inability of the colonists to get the power to issue their own money permanently out of the hands of George III and international bankers was the prime reason for the Revolutionary War.[89]

Franklin was one of the first printers of colonial script, a non-interest-bearing currency used to enable trade. Before this script was printed, beads and tobacco leaves were used. The colonies thrived using this system. Non-interest-bearing script is usury-free money. It is released into the population according to the population size and need. All businesses agree to accept it in trade. No banks charge interest on it; it just is.

Officials of the Bank of England were threatened by the existence of this system and pressured the king to end its practice. English law put an end to colonial script. Non-interest-bearing money is the original honor-bound, Biblical, intent of money creation.

Money created out of nothing was key to the birth of the United States. The ability to create money is the essence of a self-sufficient economy. Money creation, colonials found out, can be tricky. The Revolution was paid for with "continentals," the name given to the new nation's first official note issuance. By the end of the war, the phrase "not worth a continental" indicated the colonies' first experience of inflation that completely devalued a currency. Overprinting of the continental made it worthless.[90] The key to money creation is printing just enough to enable trade according to needs of a population. This is power in a very real sense.

When England took away colonial money, the colonies experienced joblessness, failed businesses, and depression. No depression or what is now called recession has ever happened without deliberate retraction of the money supply. Economic crashes and slumps are man-made phenomena brought on by a retraction of the money supply. Those in charge of the issuance of money are directly responsible for economic crashes. Conversely, overinflating the money supply creates economic booms.

The question of who would wield the Money Power and how they were going to do it inspired the first serious political fighting in US history. The battle started on the floor of the Constitutional Convention and continued throughout the first hundred years of the United States' existence.

In the early days of the Republic, Thomas Jefferson and Alexander Hamilton were archenemies on the money issue. The stakes involved establishing a central bank of the United States.[91] Jefferson was against a central bank. He saw a monopoly on currency creation as a great evil that had the power to enslave the people and rob them of their homes and autonomy. He fought for decentralized banking; his vision was that each state should hold and control the power for bank creation and currency oversight as it saw fit.

Hamilton, on the other hand, saw a debt-based national central bank as a way to control the "great beast"—his term for Jefferson's "people," the common masses — and bring order to society. Hamilton fought to establish a system modeled after the Bank of England that would be able to amass capital for trade and economic growth on a scale to compete on the world stage. Jefferson saw Hamilton's vision as a reflection of the root of all the evil Americans had just escaped.

The politics around allowing a central bank power over local banks were explosive. Decisions on the way money would be created and exchanged among the states inspired high voter turnout throughout the first century of the existence of the United States. Control of the creation of money directly relates to our freedom to master our own lives and create the existence we choose to live. Those who control the creation of money hold control of our nation's honor.

How the money we create works, the honor that backs its value, has a direct impact on our state of existence, both materially and spiritually. The way money works in the United States is not a conservative or a liberal issue. Money Power is an American issue. How money works is hidden behind obscure economic language. This obscure language is enough to undermine the highest of intelligences.

We need to understand that a healthy economy, one aligned with the Absolutes, depends on a stable and honest money supply. In the distant past, a stable and honest money supply meant the absence of usury. In more recent history, a stable and honest money supply meant every dollar correlated to actual gold bullion in a vault. An unstable money supply—an "elastic" money supply is what economists like to call it—is one in which the printing of money is subject to the actions of politicians and bankers.

Today the United States has an elastic money supply. The automobile manufacturing industrialist Henry Ford said, "It is well enough that the people of the nation do not understand our banking and monetary system, for if they did, I believe there would be a revolution before tomorrow morning."[92] Henry Ford had some misguided notions about Jews and money, and these misguided notions fueled the Nazis. Nonetheless, we do not have a stable or an honest money supply in the United States of America today, and most citizens are completely unaware of the dishonesty they support.

The Money Power controls most of our media and most of our politicians. We need to pay attention to the voices that are not championed by the mainstream media. For example, pay attention to the things said by Ron Paul, Republican Congressman from Texas. He is calling for an honest money supply; he wants to dismantle the Federal Reserve system. There is an organization called Restore the Republic[93] which runs a radio station and publishes a monthly journal dedicated to restoring our nation to Constitutional mandate. Listen and watch for people who are championing a return to constitutional money. The interest and support for constitutional money is building. You have to look for it.

For me, discovering Eustace Mullins' *The Secrets of the Federal Reserve* and reading supporting books have been transforming experiences.[94] But, admittedly, evidence of both extreme corruption and monetary abuse as norms in establishing the Federal Reserve dollar as the world's reserve currency is not easy to absorb.

Mullins and the others lay out the operations of a revolutionary debt-based Money Power movement hatched in 1773! Over the last two centuries, this movement has created economic conditions that reduced the masses to starvation and unemployment. The Money Power used propaganda to instill outrage and direct hate toward existing ruling classes so that the new debt-based system could take over the world's money supply. Every war the United States has entered into is cast in an entirely new light as a result.

I found myself rejecting the evidence, but the facts didn't go away. The more I read about the workings of the Money Power in the world today, the way money is pegged to the dollar, the way nations are hooked into debt to the World Bank, the more I saw the work of Mullins and others reflected in reality. I needed to understand how we got to this place. I needed to get to how our accepted monetary system took form.

I discovered that the model for the modern operation of dishonest money began in the 1100s in England when goldsmiths, who became more commonly known as money changers, controlled the creation of "notes." These notes vouched for the existence of gold in the goldsmith's care. This gold was held in the name of the note holder, who could trade the notes for goods. The note could be redeemed for gold at any time.

Goldsmiths discovered they could issue more notes on the gold in their care than there was actual gold and make money on the "inflation" without detection because the owners of the gold never redeemed all their notes at the same time. The goldsmiths also discovered that by creating surplus notes (currency) they could create investment booms and that by retracting those notes from circulation they could amass fortunes when debtors were forced into default for lack of available funds.[95] In this same era, usury became widely practiced in Christian circles.

Many people think exorbitant interest is usury. This is not correct. Any interest charged on money is usury. Any profit made from loaning or exchanging money that doesn't involve creation of work or a material value exchange is usury. The exorbitant interest idea comes from the Church's desire to find a way around biblical law. The Church created the "purgatory" doctrine to deal with the the fact that the practice of usury was forbidden by God even though it enabled trade and social growth. Usury was declared a sin that would require time spent in purgatory before acceptance into heaven after death.[96] Charging exorbitant interest became the sin that could get you eternal damnation.

From the conflict between Thomas Jefferson and Alexander Hamilton to the work of Roger Sherman, it seems clear to me that the founding fathers were fully conscious of the workings of the debt-based Money Power as well as the insidious consequences of money creation. One of the primary reasons they created the Constitution was to clarify how notes would work in the new nation. Private bankers alone were given the power to create notes. Government was not given the authority to create notes.

According to the Constitution, the federal government can set the value of gold and silver coin and coin any gold or silver brought to it. States are constitutionally restricted from creating notes. States have the right to set guidelines for bank creation of the notes. States have the authority to set laws assigning value to the notes. To ensure that the states stay honest, thanks to Roger Sherman, the Constitution requires that all taxes and state debts can only be paid in silver and gold in values prescribed by the federal government. States are bound by Article 1 Section 10 of the Constitution which says that no state shall "emit Bills of Credit; make any Thing but gold and silver Coin a Tender in Payment of Debts."

Well into the 1860s, only gold and silver counted as legal tender for taxes and payments of government debt. Today, the US Treasury calls Federal Reserve notes legal tender, but according to the Constitution they are not. A state can agree to take them for payment of debts. And we can agree to accept them as payment of debt or we can accept them as salary from the state, but the state cannot make us do so.[97] Article 1 Section 10 of the Constitution has never been repealed. Yet we do not have gold and silver coins in circulation or even currency which is backed by gold or silver.

We the People have not been paying attention. Our money supply is not what it should be according to the law of our land. We do not have an honest or stable money supply. We need to understand this very important fact of our lives. Sovereignty over our own lives depends on understanding this. Freedom from tyranny depends on us understanding how money works. Our own belief in the value of our money enables or disables the issuer. If we refuse to use a currency, the issuer loses power.

Honest money can only exist when there is a stable money supply. Gold and silver have worked as stabilizers, because the supply of metals can only increase at a very slow rate. Any metal or material of choice works as well as any other. Linking currency to anything of tangible value, anything in which the supply is dictated by nature and/or limited to man's ability to find and retrieve it, keeps the money supply stable. Gold and silver and other commodity-based currencies are unstable when they are covertly inflated, as goldsmiths learned to do.

The term "fractional reserve banking" comes from the practice that legalized the goldsmiths' covert inflation. Fractional reserve banking is the issuing of more notes than banks actually have in gold to back them up. Fractional reserve banking allows for issuing a politically agreed-upon fraction more currency than there is gold or silver held in reserve. For example, from 1834 to 1860 in the United States, the average state standard was 17.2 percent.[98] This means the banks had specie (gold or silver) in reserve that covered the value of 17.2 percent of the notes in circulation.

Fractional reserves means that it's impossible to give those with funds in a bank all of their money at the same time. The money said to be on deposit does not actually exist. In 1860, 80 percent of the money said to be in the banks' control was created out of nothing.

The practice of issuing money out of nothing is still called fractional reserve banking. But the gold to back the value of issuance is no longer required. There is no gold or silver standard. Today, banks create out of thin air the money that they lend to us.[99] Ben Franklin did the same thing when he created colonial script. The difference is today's banker is charging interest on the money printed out of nothing.

Fractional reserve banking today is based on the deposits and debts on a bank's books. Debts count as gold and silver used to. More money is printed based on the value of a bank's debts. Bankers subjectively create additional currency according to their analyses of their perceived need versus their risk factors. The perceived need is open to opinion. The risk is in continued debt repayment. Defaults on loans can bring down the entire economic structure. This is how the financial term, "too big to fail," came into being. "Too big to fail," justifies "bailouts," that is, money printed to cover huge defaults when and if necessary.

Banking law that enables "fractional reserve" banking is supported by the argument that it facilitates trade. Usury-free currency facilitated trade too. Why are we paying interest?

Bankers argue that interest rates are needed because they, the bankers, should be paid for their services in managing the money. Banks can also argue that since our money is unhooked from gold, interest rates are needed to give the money value.

Banks originally argued that fractional reserves were needed to facilitate trade because there is not enough gold and silver available for our population's needs. This argument is pervasive in economic dialogue. The lack of gold and silver in the original colonies was the reason for the creation of the notes Ben Franklin printed in the first place. Saying there isn't enough gold or silver to facilitate trade is cover for the perpetuation of the old goldsmith fractional reserve scam.

It's true that the supply of gold and silver is limited. The law of supply and demand dictates that limited supply increases the value of the gold and silver. Roger Sherman's *A Caveat Against Injustice* shows us that pegging a value on a currency ends the goldsmith scam by limiting how much currency can be issued. That is what constitutional money is all about.

Printing money out of nothing and loaning it out at interest is the game of a con artist. Corruption is impossible to resist or avoid when there is no check on the amount of money that can be printed. Politicians and bankers and government contractors get rich using the money just off the press. Their inflated wealth devalues the money of We the People.

In 1962 world renowned economist Milton Friedman called the fractional reserve scam to account. Friedman argued that if fractional reserves are required because there is not enough gold and silver to enable trade, then instead of a fractional reserve system we should print a set supply of currency based on the needs of our population's trade. According to Friedman, fractional reserve banking could then be abolished.[100] In spite of this common sense, the madness of fractional reserve banking continues. This madness is the direct cause of inflation. This madness is the direct cause of financial crashes.

Inflation, a sign of fraud, is an accepted fact of life in today's economy. The only concern expressed by market gurus is how much inflation there is. The means for measuring inflation, the Consumer Price Index, conveniently changes to reflect low numbers. The prices for food and energy, for example, are not included in the Consumer Price Index.

Modern banking practice is outright fraud and We the People are ignorant. Scan "gold-bug" newspapers and Web sites dedicated to honest money (i.e., www.321gold.com) and you will find emotion-charged writings by well-educated, straight thinking investment professionals denouncing and deriding the Money Power.

People count on the value of their money. People perceive that their money has an agreed-upon value. Bankers dishonor this agreement by increasing the supply of money as needed for their purposes. This increase in supply devalues existing money. The ability to create more money if an investment goes sour steals the value of everyone's money. Creating money to cover losses is corruption. Current Federal Reserve Chairman Ben Bernanke calls the corrupt reality of the workings of the current system a "moral hazard."

Banking and investment fraud in the form of inflated supply of currencies has been a fact of life for as long as trade has been conducted in America. The creation of money inspires counterfeiters and issuers of currency to cheat. Dishonor is the "shadow" of human nature; we are imperfect. A strict system of checks and balances is essential if we are going to have honest money.

Honest money stems inflation. Inflation was of primary concern during creation of the Constitution. Concern about inflation continued through the 1800s and climaxed in the Panic of 1907 when the public became aware that their banks could not really give them all their money on demand. Outrage built up and panics swept across the United States, inspiring runs on banks. Banks failed.

Political pressure to solve the problem led to Congress passing the Federal Reserve Act in 1913. As a result of this Act, a private consortium of banks, what we now call the Federal Reserve, was given oversight of banking and a monopoly of "last resort" for creation of money.[101] Today, "last resort" is not part of the dialogue; the Federal Reserve is the primary money creator in the United States, some might say the world.

At the time federally insured deposits and bailouts stemmed civil unrest and eased the worst fallout of currency mismanagement. But the Federal Reserve and federally insured deposits do not change the reality of inflation's existence. The value of our money continues to erode as the Federal Reserve pulls the strings in staged efforts to create a "stable" money supply.

Fortunes are made and lost on both ends of imbalance of money supply. On one end there is inflation, oversupply of money. When there is inflation, there is a boom time; money flows freely, jobs are created, and profits soar for those who get in on the new money. But inflation hurts people on set incomes. Preexisting money becomes less valuable in times of inflation. Then when inflation threatens to devalue all currency, a recession becomes necessary. The 2007 subprime mortgage "crisis" is a case in point. A deliberate retraction of the supply of money is being imposed.

Retraction is created by any one or any combination of several factors such as a deliberate stop on money being spent, the raising of interest rates or the tightening of standards for loan qualification. With retraction of the money supply, the value of existing money goes up and boom conditions disappear. Unemployment becomes necessary. Money is not available for investment. Money is not available to pay back loans. Debtors lose their homes and businesses. Debtor nations with loans from the World Bank and international groups such as the World Trade Organization lose control of their nations.

Depressions and recessions are deliberate. They result from conscious actions taken by the Federal Reserve chairman and his board and their equals on the boards of central banks around the world.

Both inflation and retraction of the money supply dishonors the sixth Absolute that is involved in money creation. Increasing or decreasing the supply of money only benefits the money manipulators. Progressives, it can be said, inflate the money supply for the good of all. Progressives insist on increasing the supply of money to cover welfare, social security, unemployment, etc. The truth is that stable money would eliminate the severe economic conditions that require government assistance. How money works has to change if we are going to solve inequity of wealth and care in the United States.

Access to the money supply should be an equal opportunity fact of life. Progressives are on the right track in their efforts to balance the imbalance in the Federal Reserve money supply. The real imbalance, though, is in the system itself. The Federal Reserve is a debt-based, usury-based monetary system. The Federal Reserve is designed to harness mankind. The Federal Reserve operates for the good of the Money Power. Causing unemployment and loss of businesses and homes increases the Money Power's wealth, and it is done deliberately. The good of all, the public welfare, is not the Federal Reserve's priority.

The most dishonorable stain on the Federal Reserve's record is the Great Depression of the 1930s, which was used to consolidate wealth into the hands of the few. The Federal Reserve, created to eliminate unstable money, was directly responsible for the Great Depression and bank failures across the United States. Friedman exposed this truth in his work and summarized his findings in Capitalism and Freedom:

> I know of no severe depression in any country or any time that was not accompanied by a sharp decline in the stock of money and equally of no sharp decline in the stock of money that was not accompanied by a severe depression.[102]

Friedman was subtle in his accusation. I've heard Friedman acknowledge in interviews his own kid glove handling of the question of the real cause of the Great Depression. The Federal Reserve has had control over the stock of money in the United States of America since 1913. Inflation hurts the value of money. Retraction of existing money, inflated in supply or not, creates severe depression and destroys people's businesses. The Federal Reserve withheld currency that was within its power to create and forced the failure of one-third of the banks in the United States.[103] The Federal Reserve's deliberate inaction consolidated wealth into the remaining banks' hands.

Federal Reserve bankers have pleaded innocent bumbling and claim that honest mistakes led to the Great Depression. I don't buy this story, but the deed is done. Thanks to Milton Friedman's work, outright depression is no longer a tool that can be wielded without blame. Even stock market crashes are prevented by the work of what is known as the "plunge protection team," a group of financial operatives charged with buying mass quantities of stocks whenever an extreme drop in the market appears imminent.[104] Public knowledge of financial workings gives us the ability to pin responsibility on money supply operatives in the event of a financial collapse.

Pay attention, because this means the Money Power is left with only war as the tool of last resort when greed and dishonesty has devalued a currency to the point of no return. War enables those who control the supply of money to rearrange their control in the chaos. War allows for an inflation of currency. War allows for millions of dollars in government contracts. War allows billions of dollars to go unaccounted for. War breeds debt. Federal Reserve banks print money out of nothing and lend it to our government at interest to pay for wars. War enslaves governments to banks. War forces economic rearrangement. War is the work of black messiahs. Military might is essential to the work of the black messiah.

We the People are not one with this work. Yet we are manipulated by fear and lies to support this work. This is the very essence of how our interface with the sixth Absolute works. Paying attention to the honor at work in what we lend our power to is how we create our very existence.

We the People, our faith, our belief, and our support should dictate the workings of our money and the creation of our nation. We the People have the constitutional power to take control of our money away from the Federal Reserve.

We have to stand with the politicians who want to do this. Listen to the politicians who speak out against corporate control of our senators. Educate yourself, and you will know that the Federal Reserve is not your friend. Write to your senators and congressmen and demand the dismantling of the debt-based monetary system that is the Federal Reserve.

You have the power to force change by the way you handle your money. Stop overconsuming. Move your money out of banks that participate in lending practices that favor overseas investment over community investment. Catherine Austin Fitts publishes a list of these "tapeworm" banks at her Solari Institute website under the title, "Where Would Jesus Bank."[105] Listen to and read what financial gurus such as Suze Orman and *Rich Dad, Poor Dad* author Robert Kiyosaki have to say. Put their advice into action in your life. Get out of debt.

The creation of money and how we honor the workings of money in our lives mirror our interface with the power of the sixth Absolute. If We the People do not maintain mastery of our money, oppression reigns and freedom dies. As the title of Milton Friedman's book *Capitalism and Freedom* implies, money and freedom are very closely related. Public sentiment, the will of the people, dictates the Money Power's power. We can take back control if we choose to. The power is with the people.

The way to taking back control became evident to me when I tracked how We the People lost control. The history that documents the balance of power between the banks and people's freedom is a startling field of political intrigue. This historical truth is stranger than any fiction.

The current Money Power of the United States gained control by manipulation of public opinion. Instilling outrage and provoking wars are the Money Power's modes of operation. Attempts to use war to gain control of the money supply date back to Jefferson and Hamilton.

Abraham Lincoln faced the greatest challenge of all in this struggle for power. The Civil War presented a major crisis in the fight against banker control of our government. In an effort to stay out of debt to banks with designs on centralizing the issuance of money, Abraham Lincoln created "greenbacks" to fund the war. Greenbacks, unlike our current Federal Reserve notes, were not loans to the American people at interest. Greenbacks were legal tender in honest form, fully accepted for taxes and debts to the government. This is a key understanding that We the People must pay attention to.

Greenbacks were not debt-based currency. Our current Federal Reserve notes are. Greenbacks were biblically honor-bound currency.

Greenbacks reflected the workings of the first colonial script printed by Ben Franklin. The current Federal Reserve notes do not. Constitutionally, money for government business was mandated to stay away from usury, stay away from debt-based currencies.

Lincoln perceived America through the Jeffersonian view.[106] Lincoln was against debt-based currency because he believed it enslaved people to the monetary system. Lincoln was against centralized control of monetary creation and issuance of currency. Lincoln did not intend to continue with the issuance of greenbacks following the Civil War.

Lincoln's assassination left the greenback currency in place. Control of wealth in our nation was consolidated into the hands of a select consortium of bankers in 1913 with the creation of the Federal Reserve. The Federal Reserve is composed of twelve regional banks. Controlling interest in these banks is owned by a handful of financial controls mostly based in New York. These controllers are the Morgan Guaranty Trust Company; Kuhn, Loeb & Company (now Lehman Brothers); and National City Bank. The Bank of England has firm control over the banks of New York.[107] The eleven regions outside of New York follow orders from New York. This consortium, over time, retracted and destroyed all Greenbacks in circulation and replaced them with debt-based currency, Federal Reserve Notes.

This triumph of the private bankers was achieved by playing on the prejudices of the people, just as the 1773 debt-based revolution's mandates for action revealed in *Secrets of the Federal Reserve,* dictated. Class differences and the public's righteous indignation regarding fraud on both the political and banking fronts played instrumental roles in US politics in 1913. Public outrage produced a wave of support for the enactment of both the Sixteenth and Seventeenth Amendments to our Constitution and in the passing of the Federal Reserve Act. Neither amendment amended a problem; both strengthened control of the Federal Reserve banks.

The Sixteenth Amendment was created in response to the public sentiment that the wealthy should bear more of the burden of providing for public works. Today, 100 percent of personal income tax money collected goes to paying the interest on money loaned to the US government via the Federal Reserve. This fact was revealed in 1984 in the Grace Commission report commissioned by President Ronald Reagan. Not a penny of personal income tax revenues is spent on public works.[108] All of it goes to Federal Reserve

Banks to invest how they choose. Our "public works" are covered by our state taxes and by borrowing more from the Federal Reserve.

The Seventeenth Amendment took away the power of state senates to act as republics and appoint senators to represent their interests in Washington, D.C. Popular elections of senators were put in place to eliminate corrupt insider politics. New York's infamous Boss Tweed was the poster child used to spur support for the amendment. However, public voting for senators didn't do anything to stem corruption. Public voting for senators streamlined corruption. Voting created politicians who answer to the Money Power that fund their campaign. Before the Seventeenth Amendment, senators answered only to their state governments.

In one year, the Federal Reserve banks gained full power to control the United States' money, politicians, and economic development. The Republic of the United States was effectively overthrown in a bloodless coup accomplished via the manipulations of public prejudices in 1913.[109]

Over the last century, rabble-rousing media-instilled outrage and political double-talk have created a false understanding of our personal Money Power. We the People have been kept ignorant about the true workings of our debt-based monetary system. We the People have a false understanding of how our government is supposed to look, work, and be.

We should not be operating under a centralized debt-based monetary system. This system defiles constitutional mandate. Control of the creation and investment of our money supply is supposed to be in our hands. Our communities, not the federal government, have the power of money creation. Yet the power of money creation has been out of We the People's hands since the days of Abraham Lincoln. The United States has been upside down since 1913.

The United States via constitutional mandate was set up to honor the sixth Absolute via the Money Power. Our founding fathers were not using my exact definitions and numbering of the Absolutes, but their intention is a clear match. War and public prejudice have been used to rearrange and dishonor the United States. War and public prejudice have put us on the path of the black messiah. War has been and is still being used to dupe us into complete dishonor.

CHAPTER 13
Question Authority

One Two Three, What are We Fighting For?

War's destruction of our honor brings us to the seventh Absolute and how it is to be honored in the Constitution of the United States. The seventh Absolute is that we must love everyone we meet.

Universal love was no more common in 1778, when the US Constitution was written, than it is today. Universal love's extreme opposite, tyranny of mankind, was and is a very common experience. Thus, universal love, the seventh Absolute, is honored in our Constitution in the dictates that limit our government's power to terrorize us and wage war. Legislating against tyranny is the equal to loving everyone.

According to constitutional law, to ensure safety against tyranny, a federally formed army can only exist for two years and then it has to be renewed by Congress. Article IV, Section 4 gives the states the power of republics in their own right. The federal government only has the right to form an army if the states grant it that right. Congress, made up of representatives from the republics that all have a stake in the United States' welfare, is the only government body given the right to declare war.

To ensure that a tyrannical dictator could not usurp the power to declare war, the states were given control of their own militias. If Congress voted to go to war, each state would have to commit soldiers and money to support the soldiers.

Full honor of this constitutional mandate would make it impossible to take seriously Country Joe and the Fish's lyrical question, "what are we fighting for?" posed in 1967 regarding the Vietnam War.[110] Never mind allow the answer to be "Don't know, I don't give a damn, next stop is Vietnam…whoopee, we're all gonna die."[111]

There is no provision for a permanent federally controlled military in the Constitution of the United States. The United States of America was designed by our forefathers to live in peace. War is against the Absolutes in the Light. War is against the Absolutes of the United States' existence. Our colonial and early American militias trained for self-defense. Our navy was our only federally funded constant. A navy was required to protect our coasts and our trade ships.

Today, the United States not only has a permanent federal military, it also has a separate mercenary army, Blackwater, that operates within our borders and around the world. This army is composed of "top gun" types, ex-navy SEALs, and covert operatives trained in past international "events." These "events" are why the United States is considered by the International Court of Justice and the UN Security Council to be a leading terrorist state.

The mercenary soldiers who work in this "army" are highly trained in specialized military operations. If they worked for others, we would call them terrorists. They work for US interests, so we call them military contractors. They operate under the corporate name of Blackwater USA. They do not take oaths to uphold the Constitution of the United States; these military men are not necessarily US citizens. This mercenary army answers only to whoever hires it. Politicians, corporations, anyone with enough money who needs to expedite "politically sensitive" operations can hire Blackwater USA.[112] As a private corporation, Blackwater does not necessarily work for the US government's interests. It works for the Money Power.

We the People have not been paying attention. Blackwater was on the ground patrolling in New Orleans during the Katrina crisis. Our

Constitution expressly forbids a standing army for fear of tyranny. Not only do we have a permanent standing army, but our money also supports a private mercenary army.

Our innate honor conditions us to believe that honor dictates the workings of our government. Our media gave the author of the book that exposed the Blackwater operation full attention, but in the face of the dishonorable forces that seem beyond our control, the media avoided challenging Blackwater's existence. It's easier to assume that our government works honorably.

It's easier to say, as Jon Stewart did on The Daily Show that the mercenaries are just highly trained guys getting a decent wage for their skills. I love Jon Stewart and I watch his show regularly, but I was appalled.[113, 114] The fact that there is an unconstitutional military force operating covertly in our nation and around the world funded by our government dishonors everything the United States stands for. Stewart treated the information as if he was unsure it was worthy of concern. A military force that is answerable only to the Money Power that funds it is a great evil. There is no honor in a military that doesn't answer to the will of the people.

Our government calls Blackwater operatives military contractors. These contractors are skilled counterinsurgents. These contractors at work in US-backed counterinsurgency operations do not take an oath of allegiance to the Constitution. They do not stand for honor. They stand for "might makes right." They protect the economic interests of the Money Power. The Money Power is not interested in "right makes might." The Money Power is only interested in maintaining profits. Military contractors are not concerned with what they are fighting for. Military contractors fight for the money. If what the Money Power is fighting for were honorable, the American people would fill the military ranks and contractors would not be required. Secrecy would not be required.

As we wave our American flags and rally to support our troops, we have to pay attention to what we are asking our troops to fight for. We the People have to pay attention to the motivation behind the wars we send our soldiers out to fight. If the cause is so dishonorable that our government pays mercenaries to do the fighting in secret, then we are not doing our job. We the People are not paying attention.

CHAPTER 14

The Enemy Within The United States: Ourselves

Changes

Getting past the United States' dishonor of the sixth and seventh Absolutes brings me to We the People's honoring of the eighth Absolute. Honor versus dishonor of the sixth and seventh Absolutes depends on how we honor the eighth Absolute.

The eighth Absolute is that overwhelming "letting go" mandate that makes life and death the same thing. The eighth Absolute is the need to stand naked when all you really want to do is hang on tight to the clothes that mask your nakedness. Honoring the eighth Absolute is what David Bowie called facing the strain in his song "Changes" in 1971.[115] Fear of facing required change locks us into a state of dishonor.

Being committed to the wrong policy or the wrong attitude when the right policy and the right attitude are before us is dealing with the eighth Absolute. We have to let die what needs to die, to birth what needs to be born. Honor in dealing with what is right, what is best for all versus what is best for self and/or what already exists, is not easy.

Eighth Absolute situations make or break us. Take energy generation. The United States belongs to oil-generated energy, and the right energy is clean, natural energy. The "right" energy generation could be solar, air combustion, wind, or a combination of all clean energies, and they are all ready for development. Sadly, the United States belongs to oil. Our Money Power belongs to oil.

A national policy that is best for the people though not as profitable for the Money Power is not easily achieved. Resistance to resolving eighth Absolute situations in honorable ways is why we have so much trouble honoring the sixth and seventh Absolutes. Resistance to the eighth Absolute causes us to dishonor the sixth Absolute. We cling to old ways of doing and creating things. Resistance to the eighth Absolute causes us to dishonor the seventh Absolute: to fight wars.

We humans fear change. Change is perceived as loss before it is perceived as gain. We fight change. We fight wars to hang on to what is and what we have. We will kill rather than embrace change.

The United States is not new to dodging honor in the face of the eighth Absolute. The way we treated the Native Americans was a dishonor of the eighth Absolute even before we became a nation. The unconstitutional formation of our federal military in the 1800s further enabled this dishonor by making it possible to kill the American Indian en masse. Dishonor occurred at the Constitutional Convention. The slavery issue was swept aside in the formation of our Messianic nation to be dealt with later.

Fear of economic ruin tied the founding fathers' hands on freeing the slaves. The prosperity of the gentlemen from the South, including Thomas Jefferson, the man who wrote the Declaration of Independence that established our nation on the first five Absolutes, was dependent on slavery. These men could not find the strength of honor to free their slaves.

The fear that comes when honoring the eighth Absolute can be overwhelming. Fear of loss of wealth is a false fear, but we humans do not perceive it as false when we are faced with it. To the Southern gentlemen of the Continental Congress, the honor involved in freeing the slaves was too great an honor to stand for. In our founding fathers' minds, freeing the slaves risked their entire economy. They could not bring themselves to dismantle an institution they knew contradicted the very Absolutes they declared self-evident. They feared financial ruin. Standing for honor was too scary.

What we face in dismantling our current dependence on oil and the energy grid way of distributing energy is equally daunting to the Money Power today. Creating autonomous energy-efficient homes free from mass distribution of power threatens the Money Power's grip on monthly energy payments. Control over people and the resources of the world drives the Money Power. Debt payments and monthly billing are their mode of operation. Assassination is a very real threat to all who threaten this system. Our founding fathers shot and killed anyone who attempted to free their slaves. The same force is at work.

Ironically, if the early slave owners had freed their slaves, they would have found that many of the newly free would experience the same fear of survival instinct and would have continued working for them. The change would have been gradual. The slaves who wanted freedom more than anything in the world would have made their way on their own. The slaves who liked having their livelihood all set would have stayed, and generations would have shifted the economy accordingly. Honor would have ruled and a civil war would not have been so easily instigated.

In the case of oil dependence and debt maintenance, the tests of honor are similar. We have to face the fact that we have no right to dictate how oil in other nations will be produced and distributed. We have to cease and desist in the prejudice that allows us to disrespect Middle Eastern and Latin American leaders' autonomy by insisting that our money printed out of nothing has more value then their money printed out of nothing. The honor involved in letting go of control over the world's energy resources and monetary workings mirrors the honor involved in letting go of slavery.

On the home front, we have to see that centralized control of the debt-based Money Power restricts development of autonomous energy efficient homes. We have to see that the "elastic" workings of the inflation and deflation of the system destroy our ability to build stable, independent businesses. The system forces us to be dependent on big business and big government.

The balance of the Absolutes happens regardless of humanity's perception of overwhelming circumstances. Financial ruin and freedom for the slaves came in the form of war. War opened up the opportunity for the Money Power to fill the honor void. The aftermath of this dishonorable action infects the way money works in our nation to this day.

The Civil War opened the door for the Money Power to take control of our nation's money supply. The public pain, the confusion, and the fear in the war's aftermath provided the perfect opportunity for bankers to establish a debt-based monetary system. Reconstruction was a Money Power boon.

We the People have to wake up to this reality. The War on Terror is about reconfiguring the oil and energy grid. We the People do not need a grid. We the People need clean energy and autonomous homes. The reconfiguration at work will not be for the good of all unless we stand and demand that it is.

We all fear financial ruin if we honor the Absolutes. Our government and our politicians know dishonor exists in the financial workings of our nation. Fear is used to control them too. But a few lone voices do speak out. Ron Paul, for example, a Republican congressman from Texas and candidate in the 2008 GOP presidential primaries, writes and speaks regularly regarding the wrong in the way money works in the US. Dennis Kuchinich, a Democratic senator from Ohio, also a candidate in the 2008 presidential primaries, speaks regularly about returning our government to Constitutional mandate.

Our Senators and Congressmen know that we have built up our national "state" in a way that would be anathema to our founding fathers. Our media blocks any real discussion of this reality. Fear of righting the wrongs paralyzes action. Fear of freeing the slaves paralyzed action. Fear of the loss of control over wealth has us killing people in the Middle East. Freedom is much more than pretty words. Freedom requires us to dismantle what holds us in bondage.

Those in positions of authority who hold to the Federal Reserve and our need to maintain Middle East "stability" as a point of honor, not fear, do so using "might makes right" thinking. In the monetary sphere of "might makes right" thinking, Hamilton used the words "taming the beast" to describe his reason for championing central banking. Supporters of this way of thinking claim that without a system of regular debt payments, people would not have an incentive to get a job and go to work. This is faithless thinking.

Having the security of full ownership of one's home and the freedom to devise alternative ways to grow and exchange food and life's necessities will not negate anyone's incentive to work.

What would be negated is the incentive to do work we have no desire to do. Jobs we take because we are enslaved to a debt-based monetary system would no longer be the norm. When we are free, we gravitate to the work we resonate with. We will always have to work. It is work that fulfills the man-made system of regular debt payments that would fall away. Working as our will dictates is part of honoring the Absolutes.

Freedom in life requires standing up to our parents and demanding our right to manage our own lives. Similarly, freedom in our nation requires citizens to stand up to authorities and demand our right to autonomy. The workings of honor in families and in money systems reflect each other.

Honor in parenthood is recognizing that our power over our children is limited to example. Honor is recognizing the truth of our limits and then guiding our children to master their power to the point of honor. I have found that not adhering to this point of honor raises dependent children. When I let go of authoritarian control of my children, they find the incentive to make things happen for themselves. Without honorable parents who let go of control, children never become autonomous adults. Without honorable parents, children spend their entire lives depending on others to take care of their needs.

Honor in the money system reflects these same workings. A monetary system that is designed to be a perpetual debt machine creates a population of people who lose their ability to survive in the world without the system. Debt-based money is a form of bondage in the Light. Without an honest and free money supply, citizens live their entire lives depending on the state to take care of their needs.

When families let go and honor each others' freedom, they open the door to joy. When a nation lets go and honors an individual's right to freedom, we open the door to the pursuit of happiness. Pursuing happiness is how we begin our ascent in consciousness. Success in our pursuit, happiness, and full Messianic power requires trust in our fellow man to be equally honorable with equal power. Maintaining our freedom means doing the honorable thing in the face of fear that others will not.

Fear that we will lose what we have if we let "others" have too dominates our operations on all levels of our society. Fear of others being equal is overwhelming. Fear of our own freedom is at work. Our citizenry and government cling to and depend on bureaucracy, government contracts, and subsidies to help us survive and to stem our fear of freedom and others.

Citizen dependence on government is a false security and a false freedom. All government can do is oppress. Big government kills freedom. If you have faith in the Absolutes, fear of freedom is unfounded. Fear of change is unfounded. You have to trust in the reality that all is good.

CHAPTER 15
Restore Our Republic

Stairway to Heaven

The ninth and tenth Absolutes tell us that everything we need materializes if we honor the full spectrum of the Absolutes as we ascend the Tree of Life. Ascending to this state of existence is what I perceive Led Zepplin to be singing about in the most popular rock 'n' roll ballad of all time, "Stairway to Heaven." At the end of this song's epic journey, we are told that if we listen very hard the tune will come to us when we all are one and one is all.[116] Messianic consciousness could not be expressed in any more perfect way.

If we resist honor as we ascend the Tree of Life, if we cling to "might makes right" in the creation of our existence and we insist on holding onto our own power to oppress others and profit from the practice, then maintaining Master status requires us to kill and support killing. Killing to maintain our reality is the mark of a black messiah.

The United States was created to be a Messianic nation. It was not created to be a black messiah. The Money Power's killing to gain and maintain power over the United States and in turn be the dominant power of the World has turned us into a black messianic force. For Christians, that makes us all practicing anti-Christs. Anyone who adheres to a "might makes right" dictate is an anti-Christ. Christ stood for "right makes might."

Killings that have maintained the Money Power's control of our nation are easily revealed in our history. President James Garfield was shot on July 2, 1881; in the interim before he died, he is credited with making this statement:

> Whoever controls the volume of money in any country is absolute master of all industry and commerce. And when we realize that the entire system is very easily controlled, one way or another, by a few very powerful men at the top, you will not have to be told how periods of inflation and depression originate.[117]

Garfield's killer is said to have been a deranged man angry about not being appointed ambassador to France. Regardless of who was responsible for Garfield's death, the Money Power maintained control.

President McKinley's assassination, one major depression and two world wars came in the years between Garfield's assassination and President John F. Kennedy's assassination. Kennedy signed Executive Order 11110 on June 4, 1963. This order essentially stripped the Federal Reserve Bank of its power to loan money to the federal government at interest and authorized the US Treasury to issue non-interest-bearing silver- and gold-backed legal tender notes. Five months after signing this order, JFK was assassinated. This order has never been repealed though the notes were taken out of circulation and destroyed after the assassination.[118]

Regardless of who was responsible for Kennedy's assassination, with his death the Money Power maintained control of the issuance of US currency. The Vietnam War and covert CIA operations around the world escalated.

Col. L. Fletcher Prouty reveals in *JFK: The CIA, Vietnam and the Plot to Assassinate John F. Kennedy* that the CIA became necessary after WWII because the invention of weapons of mass destruction took the business of war as usual off the table.[119] The business of war as usual was fully exposed by Brig. Gen. Smedley D. Butler when he spoke out in 1935 in *War Is a Racket*. Butler describes how the US military had been used to further the Money Power's control of the world since the Federal Reserve first came to power:

> I helped make Mexico, especially Tampico, safe for American oil interests in 1914. I helped make Haiti and Cuba a decent place for the National City Bank boys to collect revenues in. I helped in the raping of half a dozen Central American republics for the benefits of Wall Street. The record of racketeering is long. I helped purify Nicaragua for the international banking house of Brown Brothers in 1909-1912. I brought light to the Dominican Republic for American sugar interests in 1913. In China I helped to see to it that Standard Oil went its way unmolested.
>
> During those years, I had, as the boys in the back room would

> say, a swell racket. Looking back on it, I feel that I could have given Al Capone a few hints. The best he could do was to operate his racket in three districts. I operated on three continents.[120]

Following WWII and the creation of nuclear weapons, spreading capitalism at the point of a gun had to be done covertly. The CIA's first civil director, Allen Dulles, was a Wall Street banker with many ties to the Nazi regime and its operatives. His friend and fellow Wall Street banker Prescott Bush, father of President George H. W. Bush and grandfather of President George W. Bush, also had extensive ties with these Germans. Together, they recruited ex-Nazi intelligence operatives and directors to begin CIA operations well before they were given the congressional approval to start the CIA. The CIA is Wall Street's operation, funded by the central banks of the world.[121] We the People have not been paying attention and the CIA, a Money Power operation for foreign control of corporate currency flow, has dishonored our Absolutes in our name.

Since the CIA was founded, its mode of operation has been to infiltrate a target country, befriend educated connected citizens of that country, and enlist them in an insurgency movement to overthrow the existing government. Once the insurgency is successful, the United States assists in the installation of the new government, and corporate franchises are assigned to the "new millionaires" who assisted in the insurgency. The "new millionaires" support CIA-trained insurgents who run "mock battles," bloody attacks that are blamed on the government they helped to overthrow. Other names for "mock battles" are "false flag" operations. If our opposition is the perpetrator, we call them terrorist attacks.

Once the CIA-backed insurgency can successfully stand down, CIA economic teams train the "new millionaires" to take over and run the new government according to the dictates of the US corporations that will be starting up operations.[122] We the People have the power to stop this type of operation. We must pay attention and relentlessly demand that US-supported insurgencies be stopped.

We the People have not been inspired to stand against dishonorable CIA action. To date, these covert operations have for the most part been carried out outside of the United States. Our exposure to the truth of the operations has been mostly limited to movie storylines. Our news and political pundits cover uncomfortable truths in very limited ways.

We know, for example, that Osama bin Laden was unofficially supported by the United States in his creation of an insurgency in Afghanistan. Sixty percent of the foreign fighters who came to Iraq in 2006-2007 to serve as suicide bombers or to facilitate other attacks came from Saudi Arabia and/or Libya. Both are considered allies of the United States![123] Officially, bin Laden came from Saudi Arabia. National security secrets mask the insidious partnerships and psychological terror operations we conduct in the world.

We now have the Department of Homeland Security controlling this type of operation in the United States. How insidious and tyrannical Homeland Security will become is up to how well We the People pay attention. Honor starts with We the People. We must stand against the Money Power's operations.

Fear stops us from taking a stand. Covert operations and assassinations are pervasive in my study of Money Power actions, so much so that paying attention has made me paranoid. I get scared just reading stories in the daily newspaper. The most recent story to frighten me is the story of Chauncey Bailey.

Bailey was the editor of the *Oakland Post* in Oakland, California. He was shot to death on a street in his neighborhood on August 2, 2007. The perpetrator, a masked man, allegedly jumped into a van and fled the scene. I immediately suspected Money Power assassins. As I said, I'm getting paranoid.

My first instinct was to scan the article to see what Bailey had been working on to see if my fears were founded. I found that:

> Bailey had recently written stories about foreclosure rates disproportionately affecting African Americans and Latinos.... Bailey had also been working on a story about a bankruptcy filing by Your Black Muslim Bakery, a series of stores on San Pablo Avenue.[124]

The Money Power assassinated Bailey! My paranoia raged. Given the bloody mode of operations the Money Power maintains as a norm, what else am I to think? Bailey's death could have been an overt Money Power assassination. Bailey's death could also have been a "blowback" of the Money Power's degradation of his neighborhood, meaning it could have been gang violence.

Either way, our current money system—the way money works in our nation and the unequal way we treat each other—is to blame for Bailey's killing.

Paying attention is going to scare us. Paying attention will even make us paranoid. Take heart, "right makes might." There is power in all of us paying attention. Absolute power is on the side of right. Forces that are outside of our control will scare us. That is why honor is so revered. Honor is standing for the good of all in the face of forces that are beyond our control. Honor requires us to stand up in spite of our fear.

The United States of America is based on the Absolutes, and I want us to be the Messianic force of the Light that we say we are. Our citizens believe we are. But I have found that our government is not what we think it is.

When you hear a US government official say the words "national security," he or she is not talking about securing adherence to our Constitution and the Declaration of Independence. He or she is not talking about keeping us safe in our homes. Protecting "national security" means protecting the economic security of international corporations by protecting the value of Federal Reserve notes as the world's reserve currency. "National security" secrets are held in place to protect immoral covert and not-so-covert military action around the world that have created and enforced economies pegged to the US dollar. "National security" is a euphemism for securing continued payment on international debt to the US dollar-based banking system.

We are now experiencing the aftermath of a century of "national security" operations in South America. We have hundreds of thousands of illegal residents, predominantly from Latin America, in the United States. Many live in economically marginalized conditions without legal protections. They work round-the-clock, back-to-back shifts at service jobs that pay less than minimum wage. They have few rights. If they make themselves known to authorities, they risk deportation.

There is growing resentment of this huge population living without official recognition. Many US citizens say these illegal immigrants should go home and get work in their own corrupt economies. No one points out that our dollar dominance wiped out the wealth of their silver-based economies. No one mentions that the North American Free Trade Agreement allowed subsidized US farm products into Mexico and decimated the autonomy of that country's independent farmers, forcing them off their land to find other livelihoods. No one points to or mentions the overwhelming debt burden Mexico and other Latin American countries labor under. Debts consumed, on average, 52.3 percent of Gross National Product in Latin American countries in 2005.

The International Monetary Fund considers any nation with debt levels in excess of 40 percent of GNP to be economically unsustainable.[125] Unsustainable economic debts subjugate Latin American nations to US and international central banks for decades to come.[126] No one points out that maintenance of these debt payments to the Federal Reserve and the other world banks requires that these governments not be overthrown by their unhappy citizens. As long as the smart, healthy, and strong come to North America to work and send money home, they will not be driven to revolt in their own countries. That these "illegals" live in our country in overcrowded conditions, often working for less than minimum wage without basic legal rights is a shame on us, We the People.

If we want to stop the flow of immigrants out of Latin America, we have to demand debt forgiveness. Debt to the dollar is debt to paper printed out of nothing. Eliminate the debt and we eliminate the need for people to leave their unsustainable economies to survive.

As for the immigrants already living in the United States, if we truly honor the Absolutes then the laws we pass based on these Absolutes must shelter all people. Our labor unions did an awesome job standing up for the value of an individual's labor in the last century. If the work of a man who paints a house is worth thirty dollars an hour, it should not matter whether he is a legal resident or an illegal resident. We must stand for equality in all levels of our existence. We the People have not been paying attention. We are not being who we say we are.

Full honor of the Absolutes means equal rights for all. Full honor of the Absolutes means Americans overseas should be held to the same laws as Americans in the United States. If a job is worth a certain wage in the United States, then that job is worth the same wage overseas. Creating a system that differentiates by nations and cultures is dishonorable action. The first Absolute is that we must treat everyone as we would treat ourselves. Honor demands that we stand for our equal rights and the equal rights of all of humanity.

Realizing that the United States is not who we say we are triggered old memories for me.

My family lived outside of the United States for most of the years between 1965 and 1975. In 1968, a very emotional year, I lived in Montevideo, Uruguay. It was the year, as I discussed earlier in this book, that I came to terms with "others." It was also the year that the Tupamaros blew up a British Ambassador's car. Kidnappings and arrests dominated the local news. In 1969, my family left Uruguay. The Uruguayan IBM plant was eventually forced to close. Only in researching this book did I find out that in 1970 the Tupamaros in Uruguay killed an FBI agent named Dan Mitrione Sr. FBI, not CIA, interesting, huh?

Mitrione was a US adviser who taught the Brazilian police how much electric shock to apply to prisoners without killing them. He introduced a system of nationwide identification cards in Uruguay under which torture had become routine at the Montevideo jefatura (police station).[127]

I was only eight years old; I didn't know. I didn't witness any violence. The bombing of the British ambassador's car was a schoolyard story. Police actions were dinner table discussions. My primary source for insight into what was going on was our live-in maid. Banessa was our trusted friend. She taught me how to roll my "r's" in the kitchen. She had a professional soccer player boyfriend and she didn't support the Tupamaros. Banessa was enamored with the promise of developing the US way of life in Uruguay. Still, it was a scary time in her country, and she would tell stories of arrests. It never occurred to me that any of the civil unrest had anything to do with my family and me. We were good and loving people. We went to church every Sunday.

Celebrating that I am one of We the People is one of my favorite childhood memories. My brother and sister and I danced around our home in Milan, Italy, practicing the Pledge of the Allegiance in excited anticipation of our return to the United States in the early '70s. We understood that we were going to have to say it every morning at school, and we wanted to be ready. We wanted to be perfect citizens in the world's perfect nation. Our years in Europe had confirmed the United States was great; we had put a man on the moon!

For my family, the Tupamaro experience was conveniently forgotten. The fact that we had had to leave Uruguay in 1969 because the Tupamaros started killing and kidnapping foreigners in their fight against capitalist colonialism was out of our minds. We didn't know about the American who was training Uruguayan policemen in the art of torture. We didn't know that justified hatred of the United States was growing around the world, especially in the Middle East.

We did know the American supported Shah of Iran had a beautiful wife. Her fashion sense was celebrated all over the fashion magazines in Milan. We did not know that in 1958 President Eisenhower was advised that the growing hatred for the United States among the people of the Middle East could not be diffused because it was based on the accurate perception that we supported corrupt and brutal governments to protect our interest in the region's oil.[128]

Our mainstream media, like my family, conveniently forget uncomfortable clues that all is not right and don't look deeper than the Pledge of Allegiance. Things like the Iran-contra horror and CIA manipulations of other countries' economies are not part of the equation as "talking heads" discuss terrorist "jealousy" of our nation's wealth and our illegal immigrant problem.

In the 1980s, the Iran-contra scandal drove me to change from a Republican to a Democrat, but I trusted our Constitution. I didn't understand that money is a man-made power that can be used for the advancement of mankind through trade. It also can be easily manipulated to enslave society when the power to create it is held in the hands of a few.

The way money works in our nation has nothing to do with choosing between the Democrat and Republican parties. The way money works in our nation has to do with constitutional law, and both parties have defiled it. Change to good in our nation, returning to a state of honor, will only happen when we change how money works. Return to honest money, and we turn the United States right side up again.

The enslavement of our citizens to the Federal Reserve note has been camouflaged by monetary double-talk. Most Americans are familiar with business cycles, boom times, and recession times. Most Americans are conditioned to think these cycles are out of mankind's control. They are not. Inflation is a direct result of printing too much money, nothing more. Unemployment, depression, and recession are direct results of retraction of the money supply, nothing more. Interest rates are arbitrary decisions made by those who have control of the money.

Starting in 1913, the United States gave a monopoly on the creation of our money supply to a consortium of private banks. Since then, we have experienced 1,926 percent inflation.[129] That means something that cost $100 in 1914—a diamond ring, for example—costs $2,026 today. The real value of the diamond ring has not changed. The value of the money has been reduced. Our money is worth one-twentieth of what it was worth before the Federal Reserve took control.

You could say, "So what? Globalization is a good thing. Central banking investment has brought us great progress. It has made us the most advanced nation on earth. It has brought us the fantastic lifestyle we live. Globalization is a reflection of the tenth Absolute." You would be right. Globalization is a reflection of the tenth Absolute, the tenth Absolute upside-down.

Globalization does have many benefits. It brings us cheap product. But we didn't create the product. The money we earned from our labor paid for the product to be made in another country. You could say we earned the product. Our taxes funded the loans that built the industry in the other countries. But we do not own those industries and we do not work in those industries. The product is now cheaper to produce overseas. We have bought our own unemployment.

Capitalists do not need industry in the United States, but We the People do. We paid for our own foreclosures; we were duped into paying for our own loss of self-support. In a sense, like the

Native Americans before us we have been duped into trading our livelihoods for glass beads—or in our case cheap imported goods.

Darwin's theory of genetic dominance and "survival of the fittest" encourages support for "might makes right" operations. This is in spite of the fact that Darwin has been proven to be only half right. Forty-five percent of our genetic makeup is environmentally alterable. Violence and emotional abuse create environmental factors that degrade our genetic structure. "Might makes right" is hubris; it's a fatal flaw. "Right makes might" is the working of the Light.

In the United States today, to be one of the "superior" means to be a full participant in globalization. The financial media tout the blueprint for globalization's success as a free system open to all. Globalization is said to be a game anyone with the financial resources to ante up can join and win. People in a "free economy" have the opportunity to build empires from scratch. No one can stop an individual with the intelligence and willpower to make success happen. No one in his right mind would deny his desire to have this opportunity. Anyone can buy into the economy, buy stocks, invest; all it takes is a savvy intellect to perceive the good investment.

Who would want to deny himself the right to membership in the "superior" club?

The truth is the richest two percent of the world's adults own more than half of global household wealth while the bottom half of all households on the planet together own barely one percent of all wealth.[130] Yes, Bill Gates and select others rise against the odds and succeed. No, we do not want to deny anyone the right to do the same. We also should not continue to allow ignorance about how the "money game" is played to flourish. Innovators with life-changing ideas abound all over the world and their ideas are shelved, ignored, and undermined to preserve the current Money Power control. How often have you heard of a brilliant idea, then have the story end that it is just not profitable to develop it yet?

Profitable for whom? You should ask. If an idea is a better way to live or develop or be, we all profit. The Money Power behind the old idea is the power at work stopping new ideas. Decentralize the Money Power and eliminate the debt-based system on the government level, and real freedom will take hold.

Ignorance breeds dependency and debt. The Money Power uses our fear of being an "other" to terrorize us into unquestioning support of its parasitical control. We do not need half of what we are conditioned to believe we need. We can survive without debt. We are good, healthier, without plastic toys from China. Being debt free is true freedom. Having food, shelter, clothing and work that makes our heart sing is wealth.

We do not need authoritarian control of our money supply. Our communities' needs are met by our work. Money enables us to trade our work for others' work. Our money has to stay in our communities for our economies to thrive.

Money works in our economies much as water works in our ecosystem. Water rains down, fills our drinking supply, feeds our crops, and then evaporates to rain down again. The water has to stay in the ecosystem for the cycle to keep going indefinitely. Money works in the same way. Money is created to enable trade. It has to be invested in product creation. Products are created and then sold. The money earned from the sale of the product is spent on additional product creation. The money has to be reinvested in the economy for the economy to continue indefinitely. The full health of a community requires that its money remain at work in the community for which it was created.

Authoritarian control that moves product investment to more profitable communities is a parasite on our communities. Authoritarian control that places profit above community health inhibits individual opportunities to effect change and amass wealth.

Authoritarian control of the money supply of the world is an age-old parasite. Americans used to know it well. James Madison spoke passionately in the spring of 1790 regarding moneychangers. Madison feared that the moneychangers, the enemy the American Revolution had just defeated, would regain control and liberty would be lost.[131] We have to wake up to the truth that we are right back where we started from.

Terror is an equally age-old nemesis. Terror is a tool used by authoritarian Money Power to gain control of a nation's money supply. Terrorism was used on the first citizens of the United States of America in the 1790s. Thomas Jefferson used the term "terrorism" in a letter to John Adams to describe the supercharged atmosphere stirred up by Alexander Hamilton, who was beating the war drums and building a clandestine Continental Army backed by the Money Power of the day.[132]

President John Adams held firm against the terrorized public's demands for a war with France. By averting war, Adams avoided debt to the banks. Banks use war debt to gain control of a nation's currencies. John Adams in his reply to Jefferson emphasized that terror was used on both sides of the conflict he had to deal with.

Terrorism is the psychological paradigm used to instigate war. All sides in a war use terrorism. To have a "War against Terrorism" is to war against warmongering. We must wake up to this oxymoron. Terror begets terror. The only answer to terror is to stay one's hand as John Adams did back in the 1790s.

US authorities would have us believe there is a new threat before us in 2008. There isn't. The same threat has been before us since 1790. The path laid out by the debt-based Money Power is clear. The earth's population is on the fast track to economic slavery. We are debtors to the 2 percent of all humans who hold the monetary wealth of the world. The War on Terrorism is being used to finalize ownership. We the People are fighting for and paying for our own indenture. The military enforcement of equal enslavement of the rest of the world is not what We the People think we are fighting for.

We know that the politicians and bankers in charge of our money are not spending it on what we want or on what we need. We know that banks prey on us with offers to lend us money and we know that when we succumb, the payments can overwhelm us. The spin our media put on support for the Money Power plays on our desire to ensure liberty. We need to pay attention to whose liberty the media wish to ensure; it certainly isn't ours.

We wouldn't think of dictating to private enterprises what they can and cannot invest in or choose to do with their money. We wouldn't infringe on a bank's right to make money. But we can stop funding those that we do not support. We can destroy our credit cards. We can move our money out of the "tapeworm" banks and bank only in community banks that reinvest in local enterprise. We can put pressure on our politicians to dismantle the federal income tax system, dismantle the Federal Reserve System, and destroy the debt-based paradigm that is harnessing the Light of our nation to "black" Messianic power. Honor demands we pay the interest on the money borrowed to date. Fine; pay it in a new interest-free issuance.

Creating interest-free issuance is getting our money back. We in the United States still have the rule of law that says we not only can do this, we are mandated to do it. According to the Constitution, our states are currently operating outside the rule of law. Honor demands that we take back state oversight of our money creation and investment.

Local currencies are the ideal. Local currency keeps profit and enterprise in communities that support the currency. Local currency makes identification and exposure of corruption much easier. Local currencies are legal. We have the power to create our own currencies today. A town called Great Barrington in Massachusetts has created its own currency called Berkshares, named for the local Berkshire hills.[133] Neighboring towns are accepting and using the new currency. The reason this idea is taking root is because it keeps the community's money in the community. The Federal Reserve has dishonored the good of our nation by not reinvesting in our nation. The essential mandate for economic health is reinvestment in the economy from which the money in use is created.

For the national and international Money Powers, investment in constructive American enterprise is not as profitable as overseas enterprise and war. Investment in restructuring our energy grids to develop self-sufficient, autonomous energy-producing homes is not as profitable as playing trader games on Wall Street.

The Enron scandal is one case in point. Top Federal Reserve banks along with other

Financial houses—Citigroup, Deutsche Bank, J. P. Morgan Chase and Company, and Merrill Lynch—were all found guilty of falsifying records of loans to Enron by logging them as assets. These false records enabled Enron to produce shareholder earnings reports that reflected massive profits when there weren't any.[134] Enron stock soared. The bankers and everyone involved made hundreds of millions of dollars. The average employee who had 401(k) money invested in Enron stocks lost everything when the scandal went public. The extent of the corruption in which these banks are involved may never be known.

The Securities and Exchange Commission was investigating the banks' records. All the documents for this investigation were destroyed on 9/11.[135] They were in Building Number Seven, you know, the building that went down in nine seconds flat even though it was never hit by a plane. Clearly, 9/11 is a "national security" issue.

Whoever was behind the attacks of 9/11 probably saved the US economy. If any more bank record manipulations in the same vein and scale as Enron had come to light, investors and traders would have dumped their stocks in panic. The stock market would have crashed.

Our economy teeters on the faith placed in a confidence game. The point is we are duped into believing that banking investment choices are out of our control. This is not true.

Our income tax payments provide the capital Federal Reserve banks use. We voluntarily give away our control. There is no law that says we have to pay income taxes. The Supreme Court has ruled that the Sixteenth Amendment doesn't alter constitutional tax guidelines that dictate that direct taxes must be "apportioned." Apportioned means equal for everyone.[136] Equal is not a percentage, and equal is not based on how much wealth one has or how much money one makes. Equal means everyone pays the same. Internal Revenue Service tyranny keeps income tax law in place. Fear of the IRS coming after us keeps us supporting a lie.

Brave activists have stood against the IRS in the past. My impression has been that all have lost. What I have been amazed to find out is that a growing number of ex-IRS officials have joined the cause. They are accusing the IRS of being an illegal enterprise. The most high-profile members of this group are Joseph R. Banister, a CPA and former IRS special agent, and Sherry P. Jackson, a CPA, CFE, and former IRS revenue agent. Jackson's story was profiled in Aaron Russo's 2006 film, *From Freedom to Fascism*.

Russo's documentary proves beyond a doubt that there is no law on the books requiring us to pay an income tax. For us to be free of this oppression is going to take a nationwide awareness of this truth. That day is coming. Public knowledge is growing on the Internet. If enough outrage finally takes root, We the People will force our politicians to act.

To be fair, We the People have been the beneficiary of the Federal Reserve scam. The standard of living in the United States is one of the best on earth. Our average citizen who reaps this boon does not realize that the worldwide inflation of our money has put our economy in serious jeopardy.

Controls on the Money Power's creation of investment vehicles and regulatory safeguards that inhibited their risking the average American's wealth have been gone for decades. The American dollar, originally backed by gold, was as "good as gold." Then after WWII under what is known as the Bretton Woods agreement, the world was encouraged by a team of the foremost respected economists of the time to view the US dollar as gold and use it as a reserve currency.

Thirty-five dollars was worth one ounce of gold, guaranteed.

In the early 1970s, inflation of the dollar became obvious. International holders of dollars, France in particular, began to cash in their dollars for gold, calling us on our promise to redeem them for thirty-five dollars an ounce. In 1971, President Nixon was forced to shut the gold trade window. The dollar was no longer as "good as gold." The US dollar was in serious jeopardy.

In what some still consider a brilliant maneuver, in 1974 US Secretary of State Henry Kissinger established the United States-Saudi Arabian Joint Commission on Economic Cooperation. Under this umbrella, Kissinger saved our economy. The US Treasury and the Saudis entered into secret agreements that cycle Arab wealth through the US economy and provide US military support for the ruling monarchy of Saudi Arabia. In return, OPEC, the international oil consortium dominated by Saudi Arabia, would mandate that oil sales could only be transacted in US dollars.

The dollar was saved! Federal Reserve notes returned to their place of honor as the reserve currency of the world because everyone needed to buy oil. The exact date that the "petrodollar" agreement between the United States and

Saudi Arabia was entered into differs according to sources. The official announcements came out in 1975, but the dramatic jump in oil prices from $3.57 a barrel to $11.17 a barrel happened in 1974.[137] I venture to say the inflated price of oil was part of the deal.

To this day, media owned by the Money Power cast OPEC as a consortium of greedy oil producers milking us for more money, but the dollar is not worth what it used to be. Without the petrodollar, the dollar would not even be. We were lucky to get the deal we have.

Our nation failed to honor the eighth Absolute when we entered into our pact with Saudi Arabia. We refused to give up "slavery" again. Our leaders did not want to give up our franchise on debt-based world dominance. Fear of economic ruin makes us choose to kill first. We choose to kill to support corrupt and brutal regimes in Saudi Arabia. The Federal Reserve franchise on printing money out of nothing and lending it to the world at interest was saved by this dishonorable choice. Our economy was saved. The price we really paid was not financial; it was moral.

Our media are not honest in exposing the whole truth on this issue because it is a "national security" issue. Our military is now officially in charge of supporting a tyrannical and brutally corrupt Saudi regime. We officially agreed to become black messiahs to save our dollar. Supporting the Saudis is a "national security" issue.

Our war in Iraq is also a "national security" issue. In 1998, President Saddam Hussein of Iraq started selling oil for euros. The destruction which occurred on 9/11 and the war in Iraq since are related, but they are not related in the way we were told they were by President Bush. Both events have extended the life of the US dollar for a few more years.

Iran and Russia have announced plans in the last few years to trade their oil for euros. The United States is talking about a War on Terror that may have no end. "National security" demands that we fight this war. "National security" demands that We the People do not fully understand what we are fighting for. We the People believe in the Light. Consciously choosing to dominate and kill to protect the power of the Federal Reserve note is not honoring the Light. We the People have no reason to kill to protect the value of the Federal Reserve note. In fact, our honor as United States citizens dictates that we dismantle the Federal Reserve structure.

Our Declaration of Independence and our Constitution set the United States up to achieve Messianic power. We the People were given the power of currency creation to enable trade in our communities to meet our own needs and create lives that are full reflections of the Absolutes. We need a stable and honor-bound currency and value of exchange with the world. The Federal Reserve note is a debt-based currency that was created on a scam that dishonors constitutional mandate. We certainly do not need to kill to preserve its value. The private bankers who have control of the issuance of these notes would tell us we do. They are wrong.

A situation that requires us to war to maintain our monetary value reflects despotism. Securing our freedom from Absolute despotism is our mandate:

> whenever any form of government becomes destructive to these ends (the first four Absolutes), it is the right of the people to alter or to abolish it, and to institute new government, laying its foundation on such principles and organizing its powers in such form, as to them shall seem most likely to effect their safety and happiness.

We the People are a "national security risk" because our mandate under our own Declaration of Independence is that we overthrow our own government when it acts despotically. From past behavior, we can be sure the Money Power will kill us before it will let us dismantle it.

According to Supreme Court Justices Sandra Day O'Connor and Stephen G. Breyer, the precedent for changing existing laws is: first, the law must be wrong, and second, it must be causing more harm to keep than it would cause to change.[138] The creation of the Federal Reserve has come to just such an impasse. We can either do what is necessary to transcend via the eighth Absolute and dismantle our current monetary system and the laws that support it or we can continue in the direction of terror and counterterror, and war our way into the future. We must decide if we are the United States of America or the International Federal Reserve fighting to be the International Monetary Fund.

We the People have to stand up for what is right. We the People have to support the men and women already working to dismantle the Federal Reserve or it will never happen. We have to demand that our politicians focus on changing the way money works in our nation. No other wrong in our nation or world is going to be put right until we change the way money works.

I believe in the Absolutes. I also believe that if we choose to be the United States of America living as our Constitution dictates, we will achieve the ninth and tenth Absolutes. The ninth and tenth Absolutes tell us that everything we need materializes if we honor the first eight Absolutes. We the People have the power to bring the United States back into the Light. Only fear and ignorance are stopping us.

The real War on Terror isn't being fought in Iraq, Afghanistan, or any other nation. The real War on Terror is being fought inside each and every one of us. Pay attention and realize the truth of these words from President Bill Clinton: "There is nothing wrong with America that cannot be cured by what is right with America."[139] Recognize that the cure is biblical: "wash our robes so as to have the right to the tree of life."[140] Washing the "robes" of the United States means to return to constitutional mandate.

A life lived in full honor of the Absolutes is possible. US citizens have the potential to realize the promise of the Tree of Life if we honor our own law. Honor humbles us and in return provides us with all that we want and need. The force of creation provides unlimited abundance when the Absolutes of its operation are honored.

The fifth Absolute is that change is inevitable. Guiding change according to the Absolutes brought us the American Revolution. In the United States today, this Absolute is in need of attention again. Common sense demands that we return to the Light. Common sense demands that we honor the Absolutes as they are reflected in our own Declaration of Independence and Constitution of the United States. These documents are our points of honor. It is time for the United States to return to a state of honor.

CHAPTER 16
United We Stand

One Love

Getting back to the Declaration of Independence and the Constitution of the United States gets our nation back to where it belongs: naked. Nakedness humbles us. Nakedness is a point of honor. We are one in nakedness.

What I call being naked, psychologists call being in the state of wholeness. Wholeness and oneness were a big part of the 1960s civil rights movement and the parallel peace movement.

The civil rights movement called us to honor the equal power of all races. The peace movement called us to honor the right of all people to live free of fear and violence. The ideal of all for one and one for all dominated: Walt Disney had us singing, "It's a small world after all," and by the 1970s, John Lennon had us singing, "Imagine there's no country, and no religion too."[141] A one-world ideal with all human beings achieving wholeness and uniting to create a state in harmony with the

Light was the spirit of the time. It was all about "Let's get together and feel all right."[142]

The subtle shifts involved in the motivations behind one-world thinking reveal the stakes involved in the quest to realize the kingdom of God. Advocates for the power of the people such as John Lennon, Bob Marley, Martin Luther King Jr., Mahatma Gandhi, and countless other great leaders in the Light have talked about realizing the ideal of one world in which all of God's children live in peace. Just as passionately, the great bankers and corporate state advocates of the world talk about globalization. The differences between the two camps are dramatic.

The first vision honors liberty and people free to create their own economies and master their own existence and pursue happiness. It entails an autonomous state in which people are required to adhere to an honor-bound existence where "right makes might."

The second vision is a corporation-bound existence in which people operate for and with a globally sponsored debt-based currency system that's maintained and enforced militarily. This commerce-bound world requires the maintenance of cash flow and profits to enable the growth of wealth. This existence is maintained by force, or "might makes right."

Both ideals unify the world. Both claim to make the world a better place for mankind. Yet one depends on complete freedom of the individual and the other depends on complete control of the individual. With real freedom, unification of these two ideals is possible.

Honoring the equality of currencies and the autonomy of individuals, communities, and nations is real freedom. Freedom to see better ways and to have the means to develop these ways is essential to liberty. The means to develop new ways is why decentralized currencies are essential. Without decentralized currencies the individual is blocked from realizing development that competes with established norms. The ability for the individual to compete with big business is the most important ideal at stake in US politics. Clear definition and knowledge of the fighting lines in this political realm have become obscured.

It is easy to see the influence corporate lobbyists and campaign money have over our politicians. There is a movement at work to have our government fund election campaigns in an effort to stem corporate influence. This is where the obscurity in the fighting lines exists. To have the government fund campaigns would be a win-win solution for the Money Power. Instead of having to raise funds and pay for campaigns to influence the public in elections, the banks that own the corporations could just print the money and reinvest the interest they earn on it in the corporations. The way money works would remain unchanged. Corporate interests would remain sovereign because our government would still have to answer to the banks that own both the corporations and the government's debt.

If we are going to free our government from being required to answer to the Money Power, we have to break up the monopoly on the issuance of money. We want our government answerable to We the People. That means the People have to control the issuance of the money. This is the reason the Constitution gives each state the authority to develop its own Money Power. This is the reason gold and silver, ore found in the ground, are the base values of constitutional money. Anyone with gold and silver has the constitutional right to bring it to the US Mint and have it coined into legal tender. We the People have not demanded that our government adhere to the rule of law.

Politicians justify the existing Money Power and preferential treatment for corporations by highlighting the great good that corporations do for the people. Corporations provide inexpensive product, which improves We the People's quality of life. But inexpensive product does not make up for lost innovation and alternative developments of energy creation and product development blocked for the good of existing industry. Blocking innovation is common history in the workings of the US Money Power. Blocking innovation maintains the monopoly. American politics are designed to "maintain economic stability." American politics, if they were true to the Absolutes as originally intended, should be working for economic vitality via constant change and innovation.

The motivation of corporations is profit, and profit is not what is best for We the People. Placing profits and status quo over the good of the people has become the "American way." We have been conditioned to shrug it off and carry on, often hoping that someday what we really want will be profitable enough for the Money Power to develop. Real good for the people, healthy communities, and autonomous enterprise have become frozen needs. Apathy has crept in, in spite of John Lennon having said, "Apathy isn't it and we've got to do something."[143]

The loss of my apathy has felt like someone ripping off my bedcovers on a frigid winter morning. Paying attention is not comfortable.

I'm especially uncomfortable with the realization that all that I have perceived as right in my birth family's way of life, our prosperity as an IBM family, our adherence to the corporate way of life, and the way our government has manipulated our nation into a corporate state backed by military might are directly responsible for all that is wrong in the United States and much of the world today.

The corporate state has brought prosperity to my family and much of the world. No one in my family and none of the individuals who do corporate work is evil. What is evil is putting the requirements of the corporate work environment before the attention needs of the family and the community. What is evil is the "might makes right" mentality that puts the interests of the Money Power and the corporations before all other interests of the state. A corporate state backed by military might desecrates our founding fathers' intention.

I'm conditioned to reject the notion of the US having anything to do with things as ignoble and insidious as a corporate state and fascist rule since either would be counter to everything the United States is supposed to stand for. We the People have been conditioned to think of Nazi death camps as the definition of fascism. Hitler was a fascist. He was also a Nazi. Nazism produced death camps; fascism didn't. Death camps were Hitler's "terror tool." Nazism and fascism are not the same things.

> Fascism is:
> a political philosophy, movement, or regime (as that of the Fascisti) that exalts nation and often race above the individual and that stands for a centralized autocratic government headed by a dictatorial leader, severe economic and social regimentation, and forcible suppression of opposition.[144]

> Nazism is:
> the body of political and economic doctrines held and put into effect by the Nazis in Germany from 1933 to 1945 including the totalitarian principle of government, predominance of especially Germanic groups assumed to be racially superior, and supremacy of the führer.[145]

Nazism was defeated, but fascism has survived. The US military fighting to protect corporate interests has supported many fascist states over the decades. Developing a one-world debt-based currency requires fascist oversight.

The fascist policy behind Nazism gets the credit for bringing Germany back to economic prosperity after WWI. That is why our central bank, corporations, military, and the CIA mirror a fascist policy to this day. Prosperity is why We the People have succumbed to supporting fascism in our lives.

Fascist thinking is an integral part of US history and it has worked well for the US Money Power. We need to understand this if we want to counter fascism. The current Money Power is a centralized autocratic force in the politics of the United States. The current US government is but a dictator away from becoming a fascist state. I am seriously disturbed by this insight. The history that supports it is very uncomfortable to absorb.

Both sides in WWII were funded by affiliated central banks. Prescott Bush, grandfather to our current president, was a front for the Nazi financier Fritz Thyssen. Bush worked for Brown Brothers Harriman, a securities group that handled all of Thyssen's accounts in the United States.

He and the Harrimans made a fortune investing in German steel and mining interests that helped build the Nazi regime. The House of Morgan, Brown Brothers Harriman, and G. H. Walker and Co., all top Wall Street financial firms, were deeply entangled in funding the Nazis. Joseph J. Trento, author of *Prelude to Terror*, says that for the House of Morgan, supporting the Nazis was a "flirtation" with fascism; for the others, supporting the Nazis was purely for profit.[146]

These same banks have funded the CIA and most of the major corporate operations in the United States since. The quest for profits has turned who we are as a nation into everything we say we are not.

Centralized bank and corporate domination of our lives usually flows smoothly, as much good does come from the dominance. When We the People protest the loss of our small towns and independent businesses, a few well-placed donations smooth out the law and shut down the protests. But people cannot be controlled this way forever. Individual enterprise and autonomous economies are humanity's preferred way of life. Fascism can only be maintained with "terror tools."

Economic instability is a Money Power terror tool. Fear that results from the loss of livelihood in economic downturns induces feelings of powerlessness. Destroyed businesses destroy the desire for autonomous enterprise. The stability offered by corporations instills compliance. Once compliance is in place, enforcement of the people's support of corporate interests is maintained with additional terror tools. The IRS is the United States' foremost terror tool.

In recent years, the United States has dramatically increased its political terror tools. The executive branch has new power to waive the rights of any suspect, citizen or not, deemed a "terrorist." A terrorist is defined as anyone who poses a threat to "national security." Adherence to our Declaration of Independence and Constitution makes We the People a "national security" threat. We are all potential terrorists.

By dictionary definition, fascism requires a dictator. However, fascism as it has evolved in the United States has not required a dictator. The centralized autocratic operations of our government and the Money Power that supports it have not been blatantly corrupt. The façade of a government that maintains the rule of law has been kept in place. Our government officials still take an oath to uphold the Constitution of the United States. Dictators only become necessary if policy becomes blatantly corrupt. Then military might has to be used to maintain power.

People do not support overt corruption unless they are forced to by threat of violence. When fascist rule succumbs to corruption, then tyranny and "terror" guided by a dictator have to be put in place to maintain power.

On May 9, 2007, President George W. Bush cleared the way for this possibility with the National Security Directive/NSPD 51 and Homeland Security Presidential Directive/HSP-20. They give the president power to assume full control of all national, state, local, and tribal government functions. They also give the president the right to take over private organizations if necessary in the event of a "catastrophic emergency." Such an emergency is defined as "any incident, regardless of location, that results in extraordinary levels of mass casualties, damage, or disruption severely affecting the U.S. population, infrastructure, environment, economy, or government functions."[147]

In the event of any such mass disruption, even a stock market crash or another hurricane Katrina, our president now has the de facto powers of a dictator. These directives do not include any checks or balances. These directives are completely contrary to everything fought for in the American Revolution. These directives completely dishonor our Constitution. These directives dishonor the Absolutes.

We the People hold the power of sovereignty in our United States. Yet unless people stand for and maintain this power, fascist dictatorship will evolve because we will cower in fear, dependent on the state and corporations to care for us, feed us, and employ us. Terror is being used to introduce fear into our consciousness. Fear lessens our ability to pay attention. Fear raises our dependence on authority. Terrorism is being used against us in more ways than we know.

Our Congress cowers as it scrambles to justify ignoring unconstitutional power grabbing by our executive branch of government. Our media collude with the Congress. Both are co-opted by the Money Power. Individuals employed by and working in adherence to corporate "national" policy depend on it for sustenance. Deep introspection and heavy decisions are easily abdicated to authorities. Compliance goes with the job. Authorities prosper when they comply with corporate lines. No one questions the ideology behind these organizations' actions. Money and profits smooth away protest from within.

Our nation is teetering on the brink of full-out fascism. The majority of our citizens don't recognize the danger. However, thanks in part to the film *From Freedom to Fascism,* and Naomi Wolf's book, *The End of America: Letter of Warning to a Young Patriot,* the Internet community is alive with awareness.[148]

My everyday encounters with individuals do not reflect this same awareness. Attempts to share my awareness in conversation have revealed to me that my fellow citizens are overwhelmed by the news media and by the senseless violence that dominates the information we are given. Liberty, high ideals, and concern for individual rights and how money works are not the average citizen's priority. Fear is.

Fear has us primed for blind panic. Our daily survival reflex is to take care of our own world and let the rest take care of itself. The word "fascism" triggers a fear-filled derision in the average citizen that is impossible to correlate with the "American way." We the People still fervently believe in the American ideal of individual enterprise and opportunity. Yet that reality is disappearing fast.

One of the shining hopes today is the Internet. The Internet is where I find people who see our nation as I see it. The Internet and book sale outlets like Amazon.com are what make the independent publishing of this book viable.

The Internet gives individuals, you and me, mass communication power.

The Internet offers us the best opportunity to counter centralized economic, corporate, and government control of our lives since the gold rush of 1849. Discovering gold gave the common man the power to develop autonomous enterprise free of the debt-based Money Power. On the Internet, individuals can develop autonomous global enterprise. Startup costs are low enough that the enterprises can be free of the debt-based Money Power.

The power to start up autonomous business enterprise is what the American dream is all about. Rediscovering the power of this dream took me back to my family history. I've already said that I've come to the conclusion that all that is right with my family as a successful IBM family is also responsible for all that is wrong with the United States today.

I'm not the first one in my family to have come to this conclusion. In the 1970s, my older brother, Bob, was an economic/political science major at Drew University. He brought home volatile ideas that ran along the same lines of those I am writing today. These ideas caused a rift in our family that runs as a subtext in our relationships to this day.

Bob as a young boy could not contain his tears in the face of the abject poverty we witnessed in our travels in South America. My mother consoled him by blaming the corruption of the governments in the countries we visited for the civil unrest and the extreme poverty. Mom assured us that the American monetary system was why our way of life was superior. The United States, Mom told us, did not suffer the extreme imbalances of wealth that countries with corrupt monetary systems suffered. The US monetary system, she taught us, was what made America great. She assured and inspired us with the idea that just by being United States citizens we had the power to change the world. A firm resolve to right the wrongs of the world took root in Bob's soul during our years in South America.

In the late 1970s when I was seventeen, my brother Bob brought impassioned outrage to our family table. As an economics major, he had discovered that my mother's answers to his youthful suffering over poverty we witnessed were not accurate. Mom had assured Bob and the rest of us, "If they get honest leaders and an honest money system like we have in the United States, they can live just as well as we do." Bob had learned that our "honest" leaders and our superior monetary system were responsible for some of the extreme poverty we witnessed in the world.

According to my brother, our father was one of the capitalist elites dominating the ignorant of the world with corporate expansion. My father stood strong for the power of progress and the common good that is served by corporations. IBM took good care of its own.

My mother returned to school to keep up with our dinner table conversations. She brought home faculty from Fairfield University's political science department to add insight into what was being discussed at our dinner table.

The most common conversations revolved around the differences between a Communist central bank owned and operated by the government for the good of the people and a capitalist central bank owned and operated by an elite few for profit that trickles down to benefit the people. The discussion always seemed to end with the fact that central banking was central banking and the few in charge of a central bank, Communist or capitalist, will always be elite. No one was ever 100 percent right. We would always stalemate on the hope that the honor and the good of all would win out one way or another.

What drove my brother's outrage and maintained the rift in our family could be neither denied nor diffused by hopes for honor in mankind. This was the idea that the decentralized power that had made the United States of America great in the first place had slipped from We the People's hands. Both equal access to capital for enterprise development and the freedom that comes with debt-free home ownership provide society's members with decentralized autonomous power. The United States was designed to provide decentralized autonomous power to the people. For this reason, the author of the *Communist Manifesto*, Karl Marx, believed the United States would evolve into an ideal state.

But the Money Power, Bob informed us, had manipulated the economy in such a way that the majority of US citizens no longer owned their homes outright. The possibility for evolution into an ideal state had been "conned" out of our control.

At the turn of the twentieth century, hundreds of thousands of Americans owned family farms outright. These farmers had never been considered good risks for banking investment. Dependence on weather conditions for stable income was too risky for debt payment maintenance. Then during WWI, these farmers amassed significant wealth supplying food to the troops. Following the war, banks rushed to make improvement loans to these newly wealthy farmers. Then came the Great Depression and drought years, and families lost their farms by the hundreds of thousands. The record number of foreclosures on American homes during the Great Depression was the impetus for the creation of the Federal Housing Authority (FHA).

Then under the guise of great patriotic fervor, the government in April 1933 for "national security" reasons confiscated all US citizens' gold. To shore up the value of "our" Federal Reserve note, no citizen of the United States was allowed to own gold bullion, gold notes, or gold coins. Under threat of a ten thousand dollar fine and possible imprisonment, all citizens were compelled to sell their gold for federal issuance according to values prescribed by Congress.[149]

My family and I dismissed Bob's impassioned information. The ban on citizens of the United States owning gold was lifted in 1974. My father's take was "So what? If the power of currency issuance is in the hands of a few bankers that we have no control over, what difference does it make?"

As my father said, "If I'm one of 'them,' the system works. We have a nice standard of living and you are getting good educations." My father also pointed out that banks had learned that home ownership is essential to the maintenance of the value of a property. Banks will never cause us to lose our homes on purpose because they need us to maintain the value of the homes, he said. Even if the Great Depression was a "conspiracy" to consolidate wealth into a debt-based system, the elite needed the debtors to prosper to maintain the system.

My family blocked my brother's message. My family kept faith in the US Constitution and our leaders' oaths to uphold it. My brother was shut out. I understood him; I listened, but I believed our system worked. I sided with my parents.

Today, a mortgage crisis is looming and the workings of our Money Power are obviously corrupt. I have no faith in my government to uphold our Constitution with confidence. Fear of tyranny, fear of what my own government is doing, has taken root in my soul.

My brother has every right to taunt me with an "I told you so." But that is not his way. For him, the pain of realization is too deep. For Bob, the message is: "Welcome to the club. There is a lot of work to be done. It is not yet too late. Raise your voice in any way you know how. Take a stand and spread the word." As Bob says, "It is time for Americans to be Americans."

We the People must wake up to the reality of our economic history and the operations of the Money Power. A fascist Money Power, a corporate state, is a multiheaded dragon that can only be slain by a population that stands for full honor in all aspects of our lives.

Humanity is flawed and so is the United States of America. The United States is the best hope and best example of human progress, but it is not infallible. Realizing the ideals of the United States of America requires citizens who practice constant vigilance. Maintaining success requires a knowledgeable populace. Knowledge gives a populace the power to rule its government.

Given that we cannot undo the wrongs of history, we have to seize the opportunities that arise to right history. The gold rush of 1849 is over, but a new gold rush exists in the power of the Internet. Maintaining equal access to and speed on the Internet is of primary concern to people who are paying attention.[150] The Internet is the global marketplace, and the promise its low-cost access holds for enabling the small entrepreneur to compete with big corporations is immeasurable.

We must pay attention to the power of creation in the workings of the Money Power. Monopolization of gold and the issuance of currency happened. Monopolization of high-speed commerce must not be allowed to happen. Get involved. Start with the Center for Digital Democracy at www.democraticmedia.org/ and Free Press at www.freepress.net/. Both organizations are actively fighting corporate moves to block and limit freedom of information and access to doing business on the Internet.

Terror is at work on all levels of our psyche. Submission to a tyrannical dictator is but one major economic crash or nuclear disaster away. We must train ourselves to resist fear in the face of a terrorist attack. We need to look at where we bank and move our money out of "tapeworm" banks and into community banks. We need to get out of debt. We need to question derisive and hate-filled messages.

We have a government led by a president who lied to us while we were in the throes of being terrorized. Bush took us to war in Iraq, a country that had nothing to do with the events of 9/11. 9/11 was a successful terrorist attack. 9/11 successfully undermined the United States' adherence to the Absolutes. If we do not pay attention, the next terrorist attack or stock market crash or catastrophic event will be used to destroy the final vestiges of what could be the United States of America.

We don't know the full history of our relations with Iraq. We do know that Hussein and his Baath party were originally elected to office on an anticolonial platform. The United States accused Hussein of committing horrendous atrocities, of ordering mass killings and torture of his people. How much he was aided and abetted by the United States in these acts is an open question.[151] We know that American-based corporations had a hand in supplying Hussein with all the elements required for his chemical weapons of mass destruction. We had a hand in helping the Iranians in their fight against Iraq at the same time we were supplying Iraq with weapons to fight Iran.[152, 153]

Hussein was ruthless in his maintenance of control over Iraqi oil interests, and our efforts to overthrow his government through insurgency failed.[154] Until the day "national security" sealing of the records can be reversed,[155] we can only guess how much double-dealing and lying is involved.

We know that Saudi Arabia and the United States have a long history of cooperation in creating insurgencies. Al Qaeda is a result of this cooperation. Osama bin Laden used to work for us. There is studied ignorance in our media's coverage of bin Laden's issues with our country.

Particularly in regards to bin Laden's reference to usury and the methods of election fraud, the Bush family has learned from the Saudi royal family.[156] We don't know bin Laden's side of the story. We don't know exactly why he turned against the United States. We don't know if he really ever did turn against the United States.

Fighters from Saudi Arabia are thought to have carried out more suicide bombings than those of any other nationality in Iraq today. Saudi Arabians make up half of the foreign fighters in Iraq today.[157] How much covert US and Saudi cooperation is involved is anyone's guess. Given our history of covert insurgency and counterinsurgency action to incite conflict in Vietnam and Nicaragua, there has to be similar activity going on in Iraq today.[158] Insurgency and counterinsurgency to achieve political objectives are established US modes of operation.

Deliberate shocks to our psychology are being created to disorient us. The history of the Money Power working in this way is well documented in Naomi Klein's *The Shock Doctrine.*[159] How, what, and where the next shock that motivates reconfiguration is going to unfold is taking form today.

Only a population operating with full intelligence is going to be able to avoid authoritarian domination when economic reconfiguration hits. Economic crisis is an illusion. Even though losing money feels terrifying, the reality is that money is man-made. Money is what we make it. Value is what we assign it. Our own fear and panic will be used to dominate us unless we pay attention. Paying attention is how we honor the Light. Paying attention is how we maintain our power. Paying attention shows us the way to constructive solutions that can be implemented to reconfigure the world to serve our needs.

A population standing united in purpose can return the United States to its original constitutional form that honors the Light. But the Money Power is not going to let We the People do so without a fight. The Money Power and those who support it use our ignorance regarding terrorism and how money works to confuse and separate us from our liberty. State corporatism is not as good for We the People as independent state republics are. Wealth is far more equitably distributed when money is decentralized.

Central bankers make incredible profits backing corporations. We the People can buy into the stock of these corporations. Regardless of this perceived equity of opportunity for superior wealth, the Money Power remains in the hands of the few. The paradigm of unlimited growth that corporations and the stock market project is not sustainable and it's not healthy. Central banking that provides the capital that makes the corporate state possible is not healthy. The entire system requires regular unemployment to sustain the value of the money and the level of profits that stockholders demand. We the People live in fear of these deliberate economic cycles that we are told are not really in our authorities' control.[160] These deliberate cycles are designed to increase corporate control and manipulate the value of the dollar. These deliberate cycles destroy small businesses and condition We the People into a state of powerlessness. We the People become dependent on the state to take care of us.

We the People do the work. We the People are the state. We the People require the freedom, tools, and money to take care of ourselves. Every state of existence reflects on every other state of existence. The state of our environment, the earth's health, directly reflects mankind's state of being. We create our reality. We are polluted. Our earth is polluted. We overconsume. Our earth is overheated.

The Industrial Revolution moved forward on the assumption that bigger is better. In truth, a network of small economic systems whose enterprises meet the needs of the specific population doing the work is far more sustainable. The United States was originally envisioned to be composed of just such a network. Each state was meant to be an independent republic with an independent economy that joins together with the other states with minimal oversight by the federal government. The people of the United States were to thrive on self-employment. The ideal state of existence is one in which independent businessmen, farmers, and artisans work together to create a vibrant and healthy community. A community that works for itself can take care of itself.

Corporations and governments will never take care of We the People as well as We the People can take care of ourselves. In *Presence, An Exploration of Profound Change in People, Organizations, and Society,* Peter Senge et al. tell us that people need to pay attention in the corporate environment because the traditional corporate structure does not operate as a natural creative force. Corporations stymie human progress by suppressing creative energy. What I call paying attention to the Light, they call being present. They recommend working on being "present," paying attention to the moment to recognize disharmonic patterns.

The corporate model is fraying at the edges because it disengages us from harmony with the power of creation: "...when the organizational immune system kicks in, innovators often find themselves ignored, ostracized, or worse."[161] "Worse" includes economic ruin and assassination. In the context of the United States, "worse" means loss of liberty, loss of habeas corpus, and the practice of torture. The bigger the organization, the harder it is to honor the Light. Fear of change makes us resist and kill rather than trust in the infinite abundance of the universe that will always provide if we let it be.

The Money Power organization most involved in world policy is the Council of Foreign Relations. Recently, I read an article on the Council's Web site by Benn Steil called "The End of National Currency."[162] Originally published in the May/June 2007 issue of the highly respected journal *Foreign Affairs*, Steil's essay calls for economists and Money Power types to face the reality of the failures involved in corporatism and globalization. He envisions an international gold monetary system that does not require government oversight! Though Steil never mentions the Constitution or the founding fathers, he calls for a return to money as originally conceived by them, money based on gold.

Steil isn't talking about freeing the world from monopolization of the Money Power or returning the issuance of money to the people. Steil is alerting those who already control the money of the world that reconfiguration is in the works and that they better start slowly buying up gold.

The price of gold has more than doubled over the last five years. If you want to save yourself financially in the aftermath of the current War on Terror, buy gold. That's what those in charge of reconfiguring the wealth of the world are doing. Even more important, get out of debt. For most US citizens, being debt free seems like an impossible idea. Debt oppression can be overwhelming. See a debt counselor and cut up your credit cards.

If you are interested in countering the goals of the Money Power behind the War on Terror and want to see the United States hold to and actually return to its original constitutional mandate that places the individual above the state, then you need to demand honor in our government. Get involved. Write your government representatives. Write to your local newspapers. Join organizations working to restore us to constitutional integrity. I've already mentioned Restore the Republic. The American Civil Liberties Union is always in the forefront of retaining constitutional rights. The ACLU is We the People's champion against tyranny. Inundate your political organization of choice with demands that action be taken to change the way money works in our nation.

My brother Bob believes we need an independent party. He is resurrecting Thomas Jefferson's political party, the Republican Democratic party.[163] The time is right for a party designed to return the US to constitutional mandate and honest money.

The time is right for change from the ground up. Individuals exercising their right to assemble can put the US back on course. This is what it means to wield Messianic power.

You can be a Messiah. Kabbalists like to say you are the next Messiah. The power is yours; all you have to do is choose to use it. Get involved and soon you will find people who think just like you with whom you can combine forces to increase your power. We have to wake up and "come together" as the Beatles once sang.

Waking up is not easy. I know. I have observed two kinds of sleepwalkers in our citizenry. I count myself a member of both at different times in my life.

The first kind of sleeper is the successful "have." The system has been very good to citizens who play the game well. A life of privilege allows us to buy "sleeping pills" to keep out anything that may disturb us. With hard work and bills paid, there is plenty of extra for life's luxuries. From this successful perspective, we see only what we want to see. Our citizens have freedom and liberty to pursue happiness. We block the atrocities our military and CIA perpetrate around the world. We wave flags with fervent patriotism. We are good; thus, our country must be good.

The second kind of sleeper is aware of the lies and the ignorance in the hearts and minds of We the People. These sleepers still believe in the ideals outlined in the Constitution and the Declaration of Independence. We don't support our government's actions that denigrate these ideals, but we don't vote or take action in protest either. We are the citizens of the United States who have not "discharged" the pain of the last century. We feel overwhelmed and powerless in the face of drug abuse, the military industrial complex, and assassinations. Our new age "experience" has been shamed into silence. We have allowed our power to be oppressed. The numbness and apathy that take root in the allowance of dishonorable behavior overwhelm us. We blame "others" for our pain and discomfort and the state of our nation.

Very few of either kind of sleeper know anything about emotional health. We just know how to stuff pain. We have failed at marriages. We have failed at self-realization. Many of our children are looking for answers we are unable to provide because our minds are blocked. We are internally oppressed. We suffer from venereal diseases, shame, and depression. We hide our experiences from the world rather than sharing and celebrating the fire and mud we have survived. It is time to wake up. It is time to recognize the truth of who we are as a people and as a nation.

Emotional health requires we reveal our personal survival stories. National health requires that we reveal our national security stories. We survived our own fire and mud. Our nation can survive its fire and mud. We are all good. All is good. Wake up. Honor is ours for the taking.

Take action to make changes happen in your world. Own your own story and act with honor every day. Be of service. If all you do is choose to smile and refuse to spread fear, you are of service. Pay attention; question all you hear and see. If you have access to the Internet, being an activist is a whole new world. Find causes that you support and add your name to their lists. Write to your local papers, your local government, and your Washington representatives.

Question authorities; question the voices on the radio and television. Call the false prophets to account. Support the men and women who are standing up for the truth. Follow up on what I have written about in this book. Find out what is going on for your self. Wake up and take action!

Awake, our American citizenry is the world's best hope for realization of one world based on the love that connects us all. We believe that everyone should have an equal right to pursue life, liberty, and happiness. Hard work and goal setting are mandatory for health and wealth. We expect our children to work and make things happen. We count on a fair playing field and honesty in government and business for our families to thrive.

We want the same for the rest of the world.

In our name, our money is being used to bring about what we don't believe in. What in past decades was the mode of operation of our covert government is now our government's overt mode of operation. Our nation is pursuing a military policy that enforces corporate expansion around the world. Military dominance is not in line with We the People's beliefs. Our government is practicing under the authoritarian "might makes right" dictate. We the People believe in honor and the liberty to pursue happiness. We the People believe in the "right makes might" dictate.

We want our communities back. We want our natural resources vibrant and healthy. We want our Absolute power. The Constitution of the United States dictates that all of these things are already ours. All we have to do is stand up and demand a return to the rule of law. Demand our money back!

Share this book with everyone you know and love. We the People can regain our power. The only thing in our way is terror. We have to see past the fear-filled noise. A War on Terror is a psychological paradigm that has no rational foundation. The only thing we have to fear is fear itself.

The time to demand that our governors, state legislators, and US senators and representatives return the United States to its Absolute form as dictated in the Declaration of Independence and the Constitution of the United States is now. It is time to get out of the mud. It is time to exercise our right to peaceable assembly. It is time to stand for honor.

Endnotes

[1] Hynde, Chrissie. "I'm a Mother." 1994.

[2] Suh, Anna H., ed. *Leonardo's Notebooks*. Black Dog & Leventhal; New York, 2005. 149.

[3] Hunter, Robert, and Jerry Garcia. "Trucking." 1970.

[4] Swimme, Brian. *The Universe is a Green Dragon*. Bear & Co.; Rochester, VT, 1984. 59: " The Universe is a single multiform event. There is no such thing as a disconnected thing."

[5] Pinkola Estes, Clarissa. *Women Who Run with the Wolves, Myths and Stories of the Wild Woman Archetype*. Ballantine Books; New York, 1996.

[6] *New American Bible*. World Bible Publishers, Inc.; Iowa Falls, Iowa, 1987. Matthew 16: 16-18.

[7] Gilbert, Elizabeth. *Eat, pray, love*. Viking; New York, 2006.

[8] Nash, Graham. "Teach Your Children Well." 1971.

[9] Peck, M. Scott. *People of the Lie, the Hope for Healing Human Evil*. Touchstone; New York, 1983.

[10] Swanson, Tim. "Triumph of Will." *Premiere*, December 2006. 91.

[11] Stills, Stephen. "For What It's Worth." 1967.

[12] Robison, James. *The Absolutes, Freedom's Only Hope*. Tyndale House Publishers; Wheaton, IL, 2002.

[13] Dawkins, Richard. *The God Delusion*. Houghton Mifflin; New York, 2006. 31.

[14] *New American Bible*, John 8:7.

[15] Illustration copyright Kathleen Farago, May 2007.

[16]Gardner, Laurence. *Genesis of the Grail Kings*, Bantam Books; New York, 1999.

[17]Cooper, David A. *God is a Verb, Kabbalah and the Practice of Mystical Judaism*. Riverhead Books; New York, 1997. 84.

[18]Illustration copyright Kathleen Farago, May 2007.

[19]Illustration copyright Tolpa Studios, 2007.

[20]Illustration copyright Tolpa Studios, 2007.

[21]Illustration copyright Kathleen Farago, May 2007.

[22]Burisch, Door Dan, and Marcia McDowell. "Emanation of the Solfeggio." April 2006. http://www.ufowijzer.nl/tekstpagina/BurischSolfeggio3.html.

[23]Gardner, Laurence. *Genesis of the Grail Kings*. Bantam Books; New York, 1999.

[24]Sitchin, Zecharia. *The 12th Planet: Book I of the Earth Chronicles*, 1st Avon Books edition. Harper; New York, 1978.

[25]Sitchin, Zecharia. "Extraterrestrials and the Vatican." www.bibliotecapleyades.net/sitchin/esp_sitchin_9.htm, 2005.

[26]Drob, S. "Jung and the Kabbalah." *History of Psychology*. 1999. 102-118. http://www.newkabbalah.com/jung.html.

[27]Chomsky, Noam. *Hegemony or Survival, America's Quest for Global Dominance*. Owl Books; New York, 2003. 189.

[28]Prouty, L. Fletcher. *JFK: The CIA, Vietnam and the Plot to Assassinate John F. Kennedy*. Citadel Press; New York, 1996. 110-111.

[29]Weinstein, Michael L. and Davin Seay. *With God on Our Side: One Man's War Against an Evangelical Coup in America's Military*. Thomas Dunne Books; New York, 2006.

[30]Lennon, John. "Mind Games," 1973.

[31]Shaw, Archer H. *The Lincoln Encyclopedia*. Macmillan; New York, 1950. 40.

[32]Smith, Morton. *Jesus the Magician; Charlatan or Son of God?* Seastone; Berkeley, California, 1998. 119.

[33]Talbot, Michael. *The Holographic Universe*. First Harper Perennial; New York, 1991. 107-8, 146-7, 127-28, 83, 188-189.

[34]Ehrman, Bart D. "From Jesus to Constantine, a History of Early Christianity." Lecture 2, "The Religious World of Early Christianity." The Great Courses Series; The Teaching Company, course no. 6577.

[35]Hall, Manly P. *Magic, A Treatise on Esoteric Ethics*. The Philosophical Research Society; Los Angeles, California, 1978. 15.

[36]Baigent, Michael, Richard Leigh, and Henry Lincoln. *The Messianic Legacy*. Dell Publishing; New York, 1986. 61.

[37]*New American Bible*, Mark 11:15-18.

[38]Baigent, 52.

[39]Johnson, Paul. *A History of the Jews*. Harper Perennial; New York, 1988. 174.

[40]Johnson, 230-231.

[41]Johnson, 235.

[42]Baigent, 155.

[43]Baigent, 157.

[44]Baigent, 152-153.

[45]Cleave, Maureen. *London Evening Standard*, March 4, 1966: John Lennon: "Christianity will go. It will vanish and shrink.... We're more popular than Jesus now; I don't know which will go first — rock 'n' roll or Christianity. Jesus was all right but his disciples were thick and ordinary. It's them twisting it that ruins it for me."

[46]Hendrix, Jimi. "Purple Haze," 1967.

[47]Illustration copyright 2007, Tolpa Studios.

[48]Tesla, Nikola. "My Inventions." *Electrical Experimenter*, 1919. http://www.teslaplay.com/autobody.htm.

[49]Hooker, Richard. The European Enlightenment Glossary, Classic Mechanics, http://www.wsu.edu/~dee/GLOSSARY/CLASSMEC.HTM.

[50]Talbot, Michael. *The Holographic Universe.* Harper; New York, 1991. 34.

[51]"TV Numbs the Brain." Raphael House Newsletter. 1984. http://www.raphaelhouse.school.nz/index.php?pid=59.

[52]Droke, Clif. *Gold Strategies Review.* http://news.goldseek.com/ClifDroke/1152542662.php.

[53]Greider, William. *Secrets of the Temple, How the Federal Reserve Runs the Country.* Touchstone Simon and Schuster; New York, 1987. 450-474.

[54]Hall. 57.

[55]Stone, Sly. "It's a Family Affair," 1972.

[56]*New American Bible,* Mark 6:1-6, Matthew 13:54-58.

[57]*New American Bible,* Luke 14:26.

[58]Hoeller, Stephan A. "Kabbalah." Philosophical Research Society; Los Angeles Seminar, Fall 1999.

[59]Information regarding UER and Re-evaluation counseling can be found via Rational Island Publishers, P. O. Box 2081, Main Office Station, Seattle, Washington, 98111, USA.

[60]Mellencamp, John. "Pink Houses," 1983.

[61]Friedan, Betty. *The Feminine Mystique.* Dell; New York, 1964.

[62]Lebow, Victor. "Journal of Retailing," quoted in Durning, *How Much is Enough?.* 1992. http://www.storyofstuff.com/pdfs/annie_leonard_footnoted_script.pdf

[63]Russo, Aaron. "Rockefeller Admitted Elite Goal of Microchipped Population." http://video.google.com/videoplay?docid=1263677258215075609

[64]Trento, Joseph J. *Prelude to Terror.* Carroll & Graf; New York, 2005. 1.

[65]Bernstein, Carl. "The CIA and the Media." *Rolling Stone,* October 20, 1977. http://danwismar.com/uploads/Bernstein%20-%20CIA%20and%20Media.htm.

[66] Ross, Sr., Robert Gaylon. *Who's Who of the Elite, Members of the Bilderbergs, Council on Foreign Relations & Trilateral Commission.* RIE;Texas, 1995.

[67] Rockefeller, David. *Memoirs.* Random House; New York. 2002. 405.

[68] Milgram, S. *Obedience to Authority: An Experimental View.* Harper and Row; New York, 1974. An overview can be found at http://www.cnr.berkeley.edu/ucce50/ag-labor/7article/article35.htm.

[69] Cone, William. "Biological Causes of Psychological Disorders." Professional psych seminar, Pasadena, California, April 28, 2007.

[70] Collins, Allen and Ron Van Zant. "Free Bird." 1973.

[71] Hall, 57.

[72] Hall, 54.

[73] Dylan, Bob. "Forever Young," 1974.

[74] Huxley, Aldous. *The Doors of Perception.* HarperCollins Publishers; New York, 1954.

[75] Cloud, John. "Was Timothy Leary Right?" *Time,* April 30, 2007.

[76] Mullins, Eustace. *The Secrets of the Federal Reserve.* Bankers Research Institute; Staunton, VA, 1993.

[77] Mullins, 56.

[78] Fitts, Catherine Austin. "Narco-Dollars for Dummies, How the Money Works in the Illicit Drug Trade." The Silver Bear Café. http://www.silverbearcafe.com/private/narco.html. Additional information also available at the Solari Institute: www.solari.com.

[79] Paine, Jeffrey. *Re-enchantment, Tibetan Buddhism Comes to the West.* W. W. Norton; New York, 2004. 220.

[80] Berg, Yehuda. "Sweetening Judgment." *Weekly Consciousness Tune up.* 27 May 2007. The Kabbalah Centre International; Los Angeles, CA.

[81] Swimme. 46.

[82] Blackwell, Otis. "Great Balls of Fire." Recorded by Jerry Lee Lewis. 1957.

[83] Simon, Paul. "Mother and Child Reunion." 1971.

[84] Key, Francis Scott. "The Star Spangled Banner." 1814.

[85] Hall, Manly P. *The Secret Teachings of All Ages*. The Philosophical Research Society; Los Angeles, California, 1977. XC.

[86] Springsteen, Bruce. "Born in the U.S.A.." 1984.

[87] Waters, Roger. "Money." 1973.

[88] Saussy, F. Tupper. *The Miracle on Main Street, Saving Yourself and America from Financial Ruin, 7th edition.* Spencer Judd Publishers; Nashville, TN, 2006. 28.

[89] Carmack, Patrick, S.J., and Bill Stil. "The Money Masters, How International Bankers Gained Control of America." Video. Royalty Production Co. 2000.

[90] Hixon, William F. *Triumph of the Bankers, Money and Banking in the Eighteenth and Nineteenth Centuries.* Praeger Publishers; Westport, CT, 1993. 78-79.

[91] Ellis, Joseph. *Founding Brothers, The Revolutionary Generation.* Vintage Books; New York, 2000. 63-65.

[92] Ford, Henry. http://www.quotationspage.com/quote/30417.html

[93] www.restoretherepublic.com

[94] These books include *The Case Against the Fed* by Murray N. Rothbard; *The Creature from Jekyll Island: A Second Look at the Federal Reserve* by G. Edward Griffin; *The Federal Reserve Board: The Wizards of OZ: The Men Behind the Curtain* by John Shannon; *Blood Money, the Civil War and the Federal Reserve* by John Remington Graham, and *Thieves in the Temple: America Under the Federal Reserve System* by Andre Michael Eggelletion.

[95] Carmack.

[96] Greider, 172.

[97] Saussy, 108.

[98]Sechrest, Larry J. *Free Banking, Theory, History, and a Laissez-Faire Model.* Quorum Books; Westport, CT, 1993.

[99]Brown, Ellen. "Dollar Deception: How Banks Secretly Create Money." *The Web of Debt.* July 3, 2007 http://www.webofdebt.com/articles/dollar-deception.php.

[100]Friedman, Milton. *Capitalism and Freedom.* The University of Chicago Press; Chicago, 2002. 54.

[101]Hixon, 178.

[102]Friedman, 50.

[103]Friedman, 49.

[104]Evans-Pritchard, Ambrose. "Monday view: Paulson re-activates secretive support team to prevent markets meltdown." *Telegraph.Co.UK.* October 30, 2006. http://www.telegraph.co.uk/money/main.jhtml?xml=/money/2006/10/30/ccview30.xml. June 28, 2007.

[105]Fitts, Catherine Austin. *Where Would Jesus Bank? (and other good folks too.)* http://www.solari.com/store/where_would_jesus_bank.php.

[106]Ellis, 16.

[107]Mullins, 92-94.

[108]Grace, Peter. Letter to President Reagan dated January 12, 1984. A summary of the Grace Commission's findings in regards to government waste. http://www.truthintaxation.us/?tax_inform=whereTaxesGo.

[109]Hixon, 181-182.

[110]McDonald, Joe. "I Feel Like I'm Fixin' To Die Rag." 1967.

[111]McDonald.

[112]Scahill, Jeremy. *Blackwater, The Rise of the World's Most Powerful Mercenary Army.* Nation Books; New York, 2007. 173.

[113]Stewart, Jon. The Daily Show, April 19, 2007. http://www.comedycentral.com/motherload/player.jhtml?ml_video=85562&ml_collection=&ml_gateway=&ml_gateway_id=&ml_comedian=&ml_

runtime=&ml_context=show&ml_origin_url=/shows/the_daily_show/authors/index.jhtml%3FstartNum%3D26&ml_playlist=&lnk=&is_large=true. September 3, 2007.

[114]Stewart, October 3, 2007. Following an incident in Iraq in which Blackwater killed eleven innocent civilians and then left the scene, Jon Stewart came on the air and said, "Sometimes I don't know what the f… I'm talking about at all." http://www.comedycentral.com/motherload/player.jhtml?ml_video=107310&ml_collection=&ml_gateway=&ml_gateway_id=&ml_comedian=&ml_runtime=&ml_context=show&ml_origin_url=/shows/the_daily_show/videos/most_recent/index.jhtml%3Fstart%3D16&ml_playlist=&lnk=&is_large=true.

[115]Bowie, David. "Changes." 1971.

[116]Page, Jimmy and Robert Plant. "Stairway to Heaven," 1971.

[117]Garfield, James. http://www.brainyquote.com/quotes/authors/j/james_a_garfield.html.

[118]Executive Order 1110. A copy can be found at http://www.presidency.ucsb.edu/ws/index.php?pid=59049.

[119]Prouty, L. Fletcher. *JFK. The CIA, Vietnam and the Plot to Assassinate John F. Kennedy*. Citadel Press; New York, 1996. 25.

[120]Butler, Smedley D. *War Is a Racket*. Feral House; Los Angeles, California, 1935. 10.

[121]Trento, Joseph J. *Prelude to Terror, The Rogue CIA and the Legacy of America's Private Intelligence Network*. Carroll & Graf Publishers; New York, 2005. 1-3.

[122]Prouty, 32-38.

[123]Oppel, Richard A. "Foreign Fighters in Iraq are Tied to Allies of U.S." *The New York Times*. November 22, 2007.

[124]Heredia, Christopher, Leslie Fulbright, Matthai Chakko Kuruvila, and Marisa Lagos. "Outspoken newsman shot dead in Oakland; Editor, reporter Chauncey Bailey was

a tireless advocate for black community." *San Francisco Chronicle*. August 3, 2007.

[125]Krueger, Anne O. first deputy managing director, International Monetary Fund, "Macroeconomic Situation and External Debt in Latin America," remarks made at the Conference on Debt Swaps for Education. Madrid; Spain. February 1, 2006. http://www.imf.org/external/np/speeches/2006/020106.htm.

[126]Greider, 485-486.

[127]Blum, W. *The CIA: A Forgotten History*. Zed Books; London, 1986. 190, 225-229.

[128]Chomsky, 214.

[129]This figure comes from July 2006 data at http://inflationdata.com/inflation/Inflation_Rate/Long_Term_Inflation.asp.

[130]Wolff, Edwin. United Nations Headquarters press briefing on The World Distribution of Household Wealth, a study by the United Nations University's World Institute for Development Economic Research (UNU-WIDER), May 11, 2007. http://www.un.org/News/briefings/docs/2006/061205_Household_Wealth.doc.htm.

[131]Ellis, 59.

[132]Ellis, 229.

[133]Malone, Scott. "New age town embraces dollar alternative." Reuters. June 19, 2007. http://www.reuters.com/article/domesticNews/idUSN0530157720070619?feedType=RSS&rpc=22.

[134]"Enron, the Smartest Guys in the Room." Magnolia Home Entertainment. DVD. 2005.

[135]Fisk, Margaret Cronin. "SEC & EEOC: Attack Delays Investigations." *National Law Journal*. September 17, 2001. http://www.wanttoknow.info/010917nylawyerwallstreetsecfiles.

[136]Russo, Aaron. "From Freedom to Fascism." Cinema Libre Studio, 2006.

[137] Zycher, Benjamin. "OPEC." The Library of Economics and Liberty, http://www.econlib.org/library/Enc/OPEC.html.

[138] "Our Constitution: A Conversation." Annenberg Foundation Trust at Sunnylands. 2005.

[139] http://www.quotationspage.com/quote/32152.html.

[140] *New American Bible,* Revelations 22:14.

[141] Lennon, John. "Imagine," 1971.

[142] Marley, Bob. "One Love." First recorded between 1964 and 1966 in Trenchtown, Jamaica.

[143] "The U.S. vs. John Lennon." Lionsgate Entertainment, 2006.

[144] Merriam Webster's Online Dictionary. 2007. http://www.m-w.com

[145] Ibid.

[146] Trento, 1-2.

[147] National Security Presidential Directive/NSPD 51. Homeland Security Presidential Directive/HSPD-20. Office of the Press Secretary, issued, May 9, 2007. http://www.whitehouse.gov/news/releases/2007/05/20070509-12.html.

[148] Wolf, Naomi. *The End of America: Letter of Warning to a Young Patriot.* Chelsea Green Publishing; VT, 2007.

[149] Roosevelt, Franklin Delano. Presidential Executive Order 6102. April 5, 1933. http://www.the-privateer.com/1933-gold-confiscation.html.

[150] Arshad, Mohammed. "Internet Firms Want FCC to Enforce Net Neutrality House Bill Would Limit Agency's Authority." Washington Post. March 29, 2006. http://www.washingtonpost.com/wp-dyn/content/article/2006/03/28/AR2006032801664.html.

[151] Symonds, Peter. "A Legal Sham: first charges laid against Saddam Hussein." World Socialist Web site, Jul 20, 2005. http://www.derechos.org/nizkor/iraq/doc/trialsad3.html: "'But in all of these crimes, US high officials, past and present, are deeply implicated."

[152] Parry, Robert. "Bush Sr.'s Iraq-Iran Secrets." *Consortium News*, May 25, 2004. http://www.consortiumnews.com/2004/052504.html.

[153] Gagnon, Chip. "Our History with Iraq." Teach-In on Iraq; Cornell University, October 22, 2002 http://www.ithaca.edu/gagnon/talks/us-iraq.htm.

[154] Ford, Peter. "Regime change: A look at Washington's methods—and degrees of success—in dislodging foreign leaders." *The Christian Science Monitor*. January 27, 2003. www.csmonitor.com/2003/0127/p01s03-usmi.htm.

[155] Clymer, Adam. "Government Openness at Issue as Bush Holds on to Records." *The New York Times*. January 3, 2003.

[156] bin Laden, Osama. Speech as reported by Al-Jazeera on November 1, 2004. http://www.informationclearinghouse.info/article7201.htm.

[157] Parker, Ned. "Saudis' role in Iraq insurgency outlined." *Los Angeles Times*, July 15, 2007.

[158] Prouty, 94-95.

[159] Klein, Naomi. *The Shock Doctrine: The Rise of Disaster Capitalism*. Metropolitan Books; New York, 2007.

[160] Greider, 146-150.

[161] Senge, Peter, C. Otto Scharmer, Joseph Jaworski, and Betty Sue Flowers. *Presence, An Exploration of Profound Change in People, Organizations, and Society. Doubleday;* New York, 2004. 35.

[162] Steil, Benn. "The End of National Currency." Foreign Affairs, May/June 2007 http://www.foreignaffairs.org/20070501faessay86308/benn-steil/the-end-of-national-currency.html.

[163] www.republicandemocracy.us.

Bibliography

Arshad, Mohammed. "Internet Firms Want FCC to Enforce Net Neutrality House Bill Would Limit Agency's Authority." *Washington Post;* March 29, 2006. http://www.washingtonpost.com/wp-dyn/content/article/2006/03/28/AR2006032801664.html.

Baigent, Michael, Richard Leigh, and Henry Lincoln. *The Messianic Legacy.* New York: Dell Publishing; 1986.

Berg, Yehuda. *The Power of Kabbalah.* New York: Kabbalah Publishers, 2004.

———. "Sweetening Judgment." Weekly Consciousness Tune up. 27 May, 2007. Los Angeles: Kabbalah Centre International.

bin Laden, Osama. November 1, 2004, speech.

Blum, W. *The CIA: A Forgotten History.* London: Zed Books; 1986.

Brown, Ellen. "Dollar Deception: How Banks Secretly Create Money." The Web of Debt. July 3, 2007 http://www.webofdebt.com/articles/dollar-deception.php.

Buchanan, Patrick J. *Where the Right Went Wrong.* New York: Thomas Dunne Books; 2004.

Butler, Smedley D. *War Is a Racket.* Los Angeles: Feral House; 1935.

Carmack, Patrick, S.J., and Bill Stil. "The Money Masters, How International Bankers Gained Control of America." Video. Royalty Production Co., 2000.

Chomsky, Noam. *Hegemony or Survival, America's Quest for Global Dominance.* New York: Henry Holt; 2003.

Cleave, Maureen. "How Does a Beatle Live? John Lennon Lives Like This." *London Evening Standard,* March 4, 1966.

Cloud, John. *Was Timothy Leary Right?* Time, April 30, 2007.

Clymer, Adam. "Government Openness at Issue as Bush Holds on to Records." *The New York Times,* January 3, 2003.

Cone, William. "Biological Causes of Psychological Disorders." Professional Psych Seminar; Pasadena, CA, April 29, 2007.

Cooper, David A. *God is a Verb, Kabbalah and the practice of mystical Judaism.* New York: Riverhead Books; 1997.

Dawkins, Richard. *The God Delusion.* New York: Houghton Mifflin; 2006.

Drob, S. "Jung and the Kabbalah." *History of psychology,* 2, 102-118. A copy and links with supporting information can be found at http://www.newkabbalah.com/jung.html.

Droke, Clif. "Gold Strategies Review." March 9, 2007. http://news.goldseek.com/ClifDroke/1152542662.php.

Eggelletion, Andre Michael. *Thieves in the Temple: America Under the Federal Reserve System.* Los Angeles: Milligan Books; 2004.

Ehrman, Bart D. "From Jesus to Constantine, a History of Early Christianity." Lecture series. Lecture 2, "The Religious World of Early Christianity." The Great Courses Series; The Teaching Company, course no. 6577.

Ellis, Joseph. *Founding Brothers, The Revolutionary Generation.* New York: Vintage Books; 2000.

Enron, the Smartest Guys in the Room. DVD Magnolia Home Entertainment. 2005.

Evans-Pritchard, Ambrose. "Monday view: Paulson re-activates secretive support team to prevent markets meltdown." The London Telegraph.UK. October 30, 2006.

Fisk, Margaret Cronin. "SEC & EEOC: Attack Delays Investigations." *National Law Journal.* September 17, 2001. http://www.wanttoknow.info/010917nylawyerwallstreetsecfiles.

Ford, Peter. "Regime change A look at Washington's methods—and degrees of success—in dislodging foreign leaders." *The Christian Science Monitor.* January 27, 2003.

www.csmonitor.com/2003/0127/p01s03-usmi.htm.

Friedan, Betty. *The Feminine Mystique.* New York: Dell; 1964.

Friedman, Milton. *Capitalism and Freedom, 3rd edition.* Chicago: The University of Chicago Press; 2002.

Fitts, Catherine Austin. "Narco-Dollars for Dummies_How the Money Works in the Illicit Drug Trade." The Silver Bear Café. http://www.silverbearcafe.com/private/narco.html. More on Fitts is available at the Solari Institute, www.solari.com.

Gagnon, Chip. "Our History with Iraq." Teach-In on Iraq; Cornell University, October 22, 2002. http://www.ithaca.edu/gagnon/talks/us-iraq.htm.

Gilbert, Elizabeth. *Eat, pray, love.* New York: Viking; 2006.

Grace, Peter. Letter to President Reagan dated January 12, 1984. A summary of the Grace Commission's findings in regards to government waste. http://www.truthintaxation.us/?tax_inform=whereTaxesGo.

Graham, John Remington. *Blood Money, The Civil War and the Federal Reserve.* Gretna, LA: Pelican Publishing; 2006.

Greider, William. *Secrets of the Temple, How the Federal Reserve Runs the Country.* New

York: Touchstone Simon & Schuster; 1987.

Griffin, G. Edward. *The Creature from Jekyll Island: A Second Look at the Federal Reserve, 3rd edition.* Westlake Village, CA: American Media; 1998.

Hall, Manly P. Magic, *A Treatise on Esoteric Ethics.* Los Angeles: Philosophical Research Society; 1978.

———. *The Secret Teachings of All Ages.* Los Angeles: Philosophical Research Society; 1978.

Heredia, Christopher, Leslie Fulbright, Matthai Chakko Kuruvila, and Marisa Lagos. "Outspoken newsman shot dead in Oakland; Editor, reporter Chauncey Bailey was a tireless advocate for black community." San Francisco Chronicle, August 3, 2007.

Hixon, William F. *Triumph of the Bankers, Money and Banking in the Eighteenth and Nineteenth Centuries.* Westport, CT: Praeger Publishers; 1993.

Hoeller, Stephan "A. Seminar on Kabbalah." Philosophical Research Society, Los Angeles Seminar, Fall 1999.

Hooker, Richard. "The European Enlightenment Glossary, Classic Mechanics." http://www.wsu.edu/~dee/GLOSSARY/CLASSMEC.HTM.

Huxley, Aldous. *The Doors of Perception.* New York: HarperCollins; 1954.

Inflationdata.com. July 2006. http://inflationdata.com/inflation/Inflation_Rate/Long_Term_Inflation.asp.

Johnson, Paul. *A History of the Jews.* New York: Harper Perennial; 1988.

Kennedy, John F. Executive Order 1110. A copy can be found at http://www.presidency.ucsb.edu/ws/index.php?pid=59049.

Klein, Naomi. *The Shock Doctrine: The Rise of Disaster Capitalism.* New York: Metropolitan Books; 2007

Krueger, Anne O. "Conference on Debt Swaps for Education" co-sponsored by the Secretaria General Iberoamericana and the Spanish Ministry of Economy and Finance," Madrid, February 1, 2006.

Malone, Scott. "New age town embraces dollar alternative." Reuters. June 19, 2007. http://www.reuters.com/article/domesticNews/idUSN0530157720070619?feedType=RSS&rpc=22.

Milgram, S. *Obedience to Authority: An Experimental View.* New York: Harper and Row; 1974.

Mullins, Eustace. *The Secrets of the Federal Reserve.* Staunton, VA: Bankers Research Institute; 1993.

National Security Presidential Directive/NSPD 51. Homeland Security Presidential Directive/HSPD-20. Office of the Press Secretary. Issued May 9, 2007.

The New American Bible. Iowa Falls, IA: Catholic World Press; 1987.

Our Constitution: A Conversation. Video. Annenberg Foundation Trust at Sunnylands, 2005

Oppel, Richard A. "Foreign Fighters in Iraq are Tied to Allies of U.S." *The New York Times*, November 22, 2007.

Paine, Jeffrey. *Re-enchantment, Tibetan Buddhism Comes to the West*. New York: W. W. Norton; 2004.

Palast, Greg. *Armed Madhouse*. New York: Plume, 2007.

Parker, Ned. "Saudis' role in Iraq insurgency outlined." Los Angeles Times, July 15, 2007.

Parry, Robert. "Bush Sr.'s Iraq-Iran Secrets." Consortium News, May 25, 2004. http://www.consortiumnews.com/2004/052504.html.

Paul, Ron, and Lewis Lehrman. *The Case for Gold*. Auburn, AL: Ludwig Von Mises Institute; 2007.

"Papyrus Berolinensis 8502." The Gnostic Society Library www.gnosis.org/library/marygosp.htm.

Peck, M. Scott. *People of the Lie, the Hope for Healing Human Evil.* New York: Touchstone; 1983.

Pinkola Estes, Clarissa. *Women Who Run with the Wolves, Myths and Stories of the Wild Woman Archetype.* New York: Ballantine Books; 1996.

Prouty, L. Fletcher. *JFK. The CIA, Vietnam and the Plot to Assassinate John F. Kennedy.* New York: Citadel Press; 1996.

Reagan, Ronald. "Address to the Nation: Tax Reform." May 28, 1985. http://www.reagan.utexas.edu/archives/speeches/1985/52885c.htm.

Robison, James. *The Absolutes, Freedom's Only Hope.* Wheaton, IL: Tyndale House Publishers; 2002.

Rockefeller, David. *Memoirs.* New York: Random House; 2002.

Roosevelt, Franklin Delano. Presidential Executive Order 6102. April, 5, 1933. http://www.the-privateer.com/1933-gold-confiscation.html.

Rosenberg, Marshall. *Life-Enriching Education: Nonviolent Communication Helps Schools Improve Performance, Reduce Conflict, and Enhance Relationships.* Encinitas, CA: Puddledancer Press; 2003.

Rothbard, Murray N. *The Case Against the Fed, 2nd edition.* Auburn, Alabama: Ludwig bon

Mises Institute; 2007.

Russo, Aaron. *From Freedom to Fascism*. Cinema Libre Studio. 2006.

———. "Rockefeller Admitted Elite Goal Of Microchipped Population." http://video.google.com/videoplay?docid=1263677258215075609

Saussy, F. Tupper. *The Miracle on Main Street, Saving Yourself and America from Financial Ruin, 7th edition*. Nashville, TN: Spencer Judd; 2006.

Scahill, Jeremy. Blackwater, *The Rise of the World's Most Powerful Mercenary Army*. New York: Nation Books; 2007.

Sechrest, Larry J. *Free Banking, Theory, History, and a Laissez-Faire Model*. Westport, CT: Quorum Books; 1993.

Senge, Peter, C. Otto Scharmer, Joseph Jaworski, and Betty Sue Flowers. *Presence, An Exploration of Profound Change in People, Organizations, and Society*. New York: Doubleday; 2004.

Shaeffer, Frank A. *A Christian Manifesto*. Westchester, IL: Crossway Books; 1981.

Shannon, John. *The Federal Reserve Board: The Wizards of OZ: The Men Behind the Curtain*. Bloomington, IN: Author House; 2005.

Shaw, Archer H. *The Lincoln Encyclopedia*. New York: Macmillan; 1950.

Sitchin, Zecharia. *The 12th Planet: Book I of the Earth Chronicles*, 1st Avon Books edition. Harper; New York, 1978.

———."Extraterrestrials and the Vatican." www.bibliotecapleyades.net/sitchin/esp_sitchin_9.htm, 2005.

Smith, Morton. *Jesus the Magician; Charlatan or Son of God?* 2nd edition. Berkeley, CA: Seastone; 1998.

Steil, Benn. "The End of National Currency." Foreign Affairs, May/June 2007. http://www.foreignaffairs.org/20070501faessay86308/benn-steil/the-end-of-national-currency.html.

Suh, H. Anna, ed. *Leonardo's Notebooks*. New York: Black Dog & Leventhal, 2005.

Swanson, Tim. "Triumph of Will." *Premiere*, December 2006.

Swimme, Brian. *The Universe is a Green Dragon: A Cosmic Creation Story*. Rochester, VT: Bear & Co. Publishing; 1984.

Symonds, Peter. "A Legal Sham: first charges laid against Saddam Hussein." *World Socialist*; article dated July 20, 2005. http://www.derechos.org/nizkor/iraq/doc/trialsad3.html.

Talbot, Michael. *The Holographic Universe*. New York: Harper; 1991.

Tesla, Nikola. "My Inventions." *Electrical Experimenter*, 1919.

"TV Numbs the Brain." Raphael House Newsletter. 1984. 24 Feb. 2007 http://www.raphaelhouse.school.nz/index.php?pid=59.

"The Aquarian Age." The Rosicrucian Fellowship. http://www.rosicrucian.com/zineen/magen119.htm.

Trento, Joseph J. *Prelude to Terror, The Rogue CIA and the Legacy of America's Private Intelligence Network*. New York: Carroll & Graf Publishers; 2005.

The U.S. vs. John Lennon. DVD Lionsgate Entertainment, 2006.

Watters, Ethan. "DNA is Not Destiny: The new science of epi-genetics rewrites the rules of disease, heredity, and identity." *Discover*, November 22, 2006.

Weinstein, Michael L., and Davin Seay. *With God on Our Side: One Man's War Against and Evangelical Coup in America's Military*. New York: Thomas Dunne Books, 2006.

Wolf, Naomi. *The End of America: Letter of Warning to a Young Patriot*. VT: Chelsea Green Publishing; 2007

Wolff, Edwin. United Nations Headquarters, December, 5, 2006, press briefing on "The World Distribution of Household Wealth," a study by the United Nations University's World Institute for Development Economic Research (UNU-WIDER).

http://www.un.org/News/briefings/docs/2006/061205_Household_Wealth.doc.htm.

Zamparini, Gariele, and Lorenzo Meccoli. *The Peace!* DVD. 2003.

Zycher, Benjamin, "OPEC." *The Concise Encyclopedia of Economics.* Indianapolis: Liberty Fund, Inc., ed. David R. Henderson, 2002. Available at http://www.econlib.org/library/Enc/OPEC.htm.

Index

www.ingramcontent.com/pod-product-compliance
Lightning Source LLC
LaVergne TN
LVHW020525100826
845148LV00010B/1341